PRAYING *the* NAMES *of* GOD

Books by Ann Spangler

Daily Secrets of the Christian Life
Hannah Whitall Smith (compiled by Ann Spangler)
Don't Stop Laughing Now!
compiled by Ann Spangler and Shari MacDonald
He's Been Faithful
Carol Cymbala with Ann Spangler
Look Who's Laughing!
compiled by Ann Spangler and Shari MacDonald
Men of the Bible
coauthored with Robert Wolgemuth
Praying the Names of God
She Who Laughs, Lasts!
compiled by Ann Spangler
Women of the Bible
coauthored with Jean Syswerda
Women of the Bible: 52 Stories for Prayer and Reflection

Praying *the* Names *of* God

A Daily Guide

Ann Spangler

GRAND RAPIDS, MICHIGAN 49530 USA

We want to hear from you. Please send your comments about this book to us in care of zreview@zondervan.com. Thank you.

ZONDERVAN™

Praying the Names of God

International Trade Paper Edition

Requests for information should be addressed to:

Zondervan, *Grand Rapids, Michigan 49530*

ISBN–10: 0-310-26307-7
ISBN–13: 978-0-310-26307-4

Interior design by Michelle Espinoza

Printed in the United States of America

04 05 06 07 08 09 10 /❖ DCI/ 12 11 10 9 8 7 6 5 4 3

To
Kathy High

Contents

Pronunciation Guide to the Names of God

Ab, Abba, Pater	AB, AB-ba, pa-TAIR
Adonay	a-do-NAI
El Chay	EL CHAY
El Kanna	EL kan-NAH
Elohim	e-lo-HEEM
El Elyon	EL el-YOHN
El Olam	EL o-LAM
El Roi	EL raw-EE
El Shadday	EL shad-DAI
Esh Oklah	AISH o-KLAH
Hashem	ha-SHAME
Ish	EESH
Machseh	mach-SEH
Magen	ma-GAIN
Maon	ma-OHN
Melek	ME-lek
Metsuda	me-tsu-DAH
Migdal-Oz	mig-dal OHZ
Miqweh Yisrael	MIK-weh yis-ra-AIL
Qedosh Yisrael	ke-DOSH yis-ra-AIL
Shophet	sho-PHAIT
Yahweh	yah-WEH
Yahweh Nissi	yah-WEH nis-SEE
Yahweh Roi	yah-WEH row-EE
Yahweh Rophe	yah-WEH ro-FEH
Yahweh Shalom	yah-WEH sha-LOME
Yahweh Shammah	yah-WEH SHAM-mah
Yahweh Tsebaoth	yah-WEH tse-ba-OATH
Yahweh Tsidqenu	yah-WEH tsid-KAY-nu
Yahweh Tsuri	yah-WEH tsu-REE
Yahweh Yireh	yah-WEH yir-EH

INTRODUCTION

When I first considered writing a book about the names of God, I felt intimidated. I hadn't spent years engaged in formal theological study. Nor could I translate Hebrew or Greek. Who was I to tackle such a subject? Yet I had difficulty shaking the idea. So I put it on the back burner, only trotting it out occasionally to suggest it as a topic to other, more qualified authors. But no one took the bait.

My previous books, *Women of the Bible* and *Men of the Bible,* the first coauthored with Jean Syswerda and the second with Robert Wolgemuth, had whet my appetite for spending long periods immersed in Scripture. The prospect of spending an entire year focusing on the various names of God in the Bible appealed to me. It promised a fresh way of encountering God. I was hungry for new and deeper insights into his nature and character.

I knew, too, that names in the ancient world carried far more significance than they do in the modern world. In addition to distinguishing one person from another, names were often thought to reveal the essential nature and character of a person. I realized this was particularly true regarding the various names of God recorded in Scripture. To know God's name is to enjoy a kind of privileged access to him. By revealing his name, God made himself not only accessible but vulnerable. Not only could his people call on his name in prayer, they could dishonor it by living in ways that contradicted his character.

So with a mixture of trepidation and excitement I embarked on the adventure that has become this book. As I rolled up my sleeves and plunged into my topic, I began to feel as though I were being swept up into a vast ocean, carried along by unpredictable currents and tides. There I found myself exploring names that comforted and consoled me, like *Abba,* "Father," and *Yahweh Roeh,* "The Lord Is My Shepherd" as well as names and titles that seemed strange or even frightening, like *Esh Oklah*, "Consuming Fire," or *El Kanna*, "Jealous God."

As I studied and prayed, God worked these names into my own life, like kneading yeast into bread. I felt challenged by names that revealed God's holiness. They exposed my own imperfections. I felt comforted by ones that revealed him as healer and provider. They satisfied my need. At times events in my life intersected with the name I had been studying. Once I tried doggedly to complete a devotional that just didn't want to be finished. I didn't realize that I had to live the ending before I could write it. That happened the next day when I encountered unexpected turbulence in my personal life. The experience brought me to tears—and to my knees. And it brought also a deep conviction of God's presence.

Though I have focused on twenty-six names of God, many of these are more properly called titles. Most often I refer to them as names for the sake of simplicity. And because I hope to write a sequel focused on praying the names of Jesus, I have concentrated primarily on the Hebrew names of God. But though I tried hard to keep Jesus out of this book, I failed utterly. How could I ignore him when the Hebrew Scriptures are alive with his presence? How could I write about *Yahweh Nissi,* "The Lord Is My Banner," without encountering Christ on his cross? How could I study *Yahweh Shalom,* "The Lord Is Peace," without acknowledging the "Prince of Peace"? Still, my primary emphasis has been to explore the Hebrew names and titles of God.

Praying the Names of God is divided into twenty-six weeks. Each week is devoted to studying and praying a particular name of God. The order of names in the book is not random but is related in most cases to where the name either first or most definitively appears in the Bible. I hope that such an arrangement will offer at least a rudimentary idea of God's progressive self-disclosure to his people.

Here's how each week unfolds:

- Monday is devoted to reading and study. It provides a Scripture passage that reveals the name, background information, and a brief Bible study to help you understand the name.

- Tuesday, Wednesday, and Thursday contain devotional readings to help you pray specific Scripture passages that contain the name or relate closely to it. The devotional readings are meant as a springboard for your own prayer. It will help to keep your Bible handy while reflecting on the relevant Scripture passages.
- Friday helps you reflect on how the name connects to God's promises in Scripture. It offers key Bible passages that can be read, reflected on, or even memorized. A section entitled "For Continued Prayer and Praise" lists additional passages related to the name that can be prayed and studied on the weekend.

An additional resource that may aid your personal prayer and study is the *Praying the Names of God Journal.* It provides an easy way to record your insights and reflections so you can keep track of how God is at work through your prayers.

Though not every name and title of God is included in this volume, I have done my best to cover the most significant ones. At the end of twenty-six weeks, I hope you will have a much deeper understanding of who God is and will also have experienced him in surprising and wonderful ways.

Though any errors or deficiencies in the book are strictly my responsibility, I want to thank several people who supported me in significant ways throughout the writing of this book. Executive editor Sandy VanderZicht has helped to shape and strengthen the book with her keen editorial insights. My friend and editor for many years, she has also been a model of patience as she responded to my requests for yet another extension on my deadline. Most importantly she has prayed faithfully for me during the process of writing this book. I owe senior editor Verlyn Verbrugge a particular debt of gratitude since he supplied both the Hebrew equivalents of the various names of God as well as a pronunciation guide. He has also made valuable suggestions and provided a painstaking theological and stylistic review of the manuscript. Thanks to Sue Brower and her marketing team for so enthusiastically supporting this book.

Their creative ideas have helped to spread the word far and wide. And lest I forget, I need to mention that the Zondervan sales team is among the best in the business. Their professionalism and dedication show through in their service to booksellers and ultimately to readers. I am grateful for the ways they have sold my books throughout the years.

To my agent Linda Kenney, I say: "Thank you for going to bat for me. I'm grateful for your professionalism and for your creative ideas, sound advice, integrity, and friendship. You are a blessing."

Thanks also to Donna Ross for her help in readying the manuscript to be sent to the publisher, and to Lucinda Poel for making last-minute corrections with so much care and patience.

I owe a personal debt of gratitude to the circle of friends who kept praying for me during all the ups and downs of writing this book: "Leslie Dennis, Joan Huyser-Honig, and Patti Swets, thank you for holding me up week after week with your prayers. I would still be writing it if you hadn't prayed!" And lastly to my friend Kathy High: "You have been faithful, flexible, and kind, willing to inconvenience yourself for months on end so I would have time to finish this book. I dedicate it to you with thanks for your friendship, and for your care for my children. If there ever was such a thing as a Proverbs 31 woman, you fit the bill!"

Whatever its flaws, I hope that this book will deepen your sense of awe and increase your faith in the God who loves you. May it be an open door for encountering him in fresh and deeper ways.

I

God, Mighty Creator

Elohim

The Name

Elohim is the Hebrew word for God that appears in the very first sentence of the Bible. When we pray to *Elohim*, we remember that he is the one who began it all, creating the heavens and the earth and separating light from darkness, water from dry land, night from day. This ancient name for God contains the idea of God's creative power as well as his authority and sovereignty. Jesus used a form of the name in his agonized prayer from the cross. About the ninth hour Jesus cried out in a loud voice, "*Eloi, Eloi, lama sabachthani?*"—which means, "My God, my God, why have you forsaken me?"

Key Scripture

In the beginning God created the heavens and the earth. (Genesis 1:1)

Monday

God Reveals His Name

In the beginning when God created the heavens and the earth, the earth was a formless void and darkness covered the face of the deep, while a wind from God swept over the face of the waters. Then God said, "Let there be light." God called the light Day, and the darkness he called Night. And there was evening and there was morning, the first day.

And God said, "Let there be a dome in the midst of the waters, and let it separate the waters from the waters." God called the dome Sky.

And God said, "Let the waters under the sky be gathered together into one place, and let the dry land appear." God called the dry land Earth, and the waters that were gathered together he called Seas. Then God said, "Let the earth put forth vegetation: plants yielding seed, and fruit trees of every kind on earth that bear fruit with the seed in it."

And God said, "Let there be lights in the dome of the sky to separate the day from the night."

And God said, "Let the waters bring forth swarms of living creatures, and let birds fly above the earth across the dome of the sky."

And God said, "Let the earth bring forth living creatures of every kind: cattle and creeping things and wild animals of the earth of every kind."

Then God said, "Let us make humankind in our image, according to our likeness; and let them have dominion over the fish of the sea, and over the birds of the air, and over the cattle, and over all the wild animals of the earth, and over every creeping thing that creeps upon the earth."

> So God created humankind in his image,
>   in the image of God he created them;
>   male and female he created them.

God blessed them, and God said to them, "Be fruitful and multiply, and fill the earth and subdue it; and have dominion over the fish of the sea and over the birds of the air and over every living thing that moves upon the earth." God saw everything that he had made, and indeed, it was very good. (Selected from Genesis 1 NRSV)

Elohim, Mighty One, you made everything out of nothing, imposed order on chaos, gave birth to beauty, and called it all good. Help me to know you as the one true God who created everything and everyone, the one who has placed me on the earth for a purpose—to magnify your name. Amen.

Understanding the Name

Elohim (e-lo-HEEM) is the plural form of *El* or *Eloah,* one of the oldest designations for divinity in the world. The Hebrews borrowed the term *El* from the Canaanites. It can refer either to the true God or to pagan gods. Though *El* is used more than 200 times in the Hebrew Bible, *Elohim* is used more than 2,500 times. Its plural form is used not to indicate a belief in many gods but to emphasize the majesty of the one true God. He is the God of gods, the highest of all. Christians may recognize in this plural form a hint of the Trinity—Father, Son, and Holy Spirit. *Elohim* occurs thirty-two times in the first chapter of Genesis. After that the name *Yahweh* appears as well and is often paired with *Elohim* and, in the NIV, the two together are translated "the LORD God."

Studying the Name

1. "Genesis" is a word that can mean "birth," "history of origin," or "genealogy." What can you observe about who God is from this passage about beginnings?
2. What can you observe about the world he has made?
3. What do you think it means to be created in "the image of God"? How would your life change if you lived with the constant awareness that he created you to bear his image?

4. God seems delighted by what he has made, proclaiming it good and even very good. How does God's assessment of creation shape your own attitude toward the world? Toward yourself?

Tuesday

Praying the Name

Then God said, "Let us make humankind in our image, according to our likeness; and let them have dominion over the fish of the sea, and over the birds of the air, and over the cattle, and over all the wild animals of the earth, and over every creeping thing that creeps upon the earth."

So God created humankind in his image,
in the image of God he created them;
male and female he created them.

God blessed them, and God said to them, "Be fruitful and multiply, and fill the earth and subdue it; and have dominion over the fish of the sea and over the birds of the air and over every living thing that moves upon the earth." (Genesis 1:26–28 NRSV*)*

Reflect On: Genesis 1:26–28
Praise God: For his power in creating the heavens and the earth out of absolutely nothing.
Offer Thanks: That God has not only created you, but made you in his own image.
Confess: Any tendency to forget that every human life, including your own, is sacred.
Ask God: To renew your sense of wonder and gratitude for the things he has made.

A mighty God could have created a world quite different from the one we know. It could have had perpetually dark skies, grass that hurt to walk on, dogs that couldn't be housebroken, and people incapable of love. Have you ever wondered why the world you take for granted is often so stunningly beautiful? So pleasant to live in? Why the people around you are capable of so much kindness?

So often we miss life's beauty because we are preoccupied by its flaws. Instead of taking off our shoes to feel the feathery soft grass beneath our feet, we complain that it's growing so fast we don't have time to mow it. Rather than enjoying the gregarious woman behind the supermarket counter, we blame her friendly chatter for delaying the checkout line. And what about us? Who stares back from the mirror each morning? A child of God who is growing daily in his image or someone whose nose is too big or too small, whose hair is in a state of perpetual rebellion, or whose skin is aged and worn?

Today, ask the God who made you to remake your sense of wonder at his creative power.

Wednesday

PRAYING THE NAME

Then Jacob made a vow, saying, "If God will be with me and will watch over me on this journey I am taking and will give me food to eat and clothes to wear so that I return safely to my father's house, then the LORD will be my God and this stone that I have set up as a pillar will be God's house, and of all that you give me I will give you a tenth." (Genesis 28:20)

Reflect On: Genesis 28:10–22; 35:1–8

Praise God: Because he not only created the world and everyone in it but continues to sustain it through his creative power.

Offer Thanks: For the way God has blessed you with the good things of the earth.

Confess: Any tendency to take God's earthly blessings for granted.

Ask God: To increase your desire to bless others with the gifts he has given you.

Jacob, you may remember, was the twin who tricked his brother out of a blessing. Fleeing from his brother's wrath, he had a dream one night in which he encountered the God of his grandfather, Abraham, and his father, Isaac. Promising him descendants as numerous as the dust of the earth, God told him: "All peoples on earth will be blessed through you and your offspring. I am with you and will watch over you wherever you go and I will bring you back to this land. I will not leave you until I have done what I have promised you."

This was *Elohim* speaking, the Creator of the heavens and the earth. He made it all, he owned it all, and he could give away its fruit to anyone he pleased. Jacob asked for safety, food, and clothing—

basic human needs. But God gave him so much more, making him a wealthy man and the father of numerous children. He even blessed Esau, the brother whose blessing Jacob had stolen.

Then as now *Elohim* desires to use his creative power, not only to sustain us and the world he has made, but to create for us a life filled with blessings, both physical and spiritual. Ask him now for what you need, believing in both his power to bless and his desire to care for you.

Thursday

PRAYING THE NAME

In the beginning you laid the foundations of the earth,
and the heavens are the work of your hands.
They will perish, but you remain;
they will all wear out like a garment.
Like clothing you will change them
and they will be discarded.
But you remain the same. (Psalm 102:25–27a)

Reflect On: Psalm 102

Praise God: For his unchanging nature—no matter what happens to us or to the world around us, God remains the same.

Offer Thanks: That our Creator is perfect—nothing could be added to or subtracted from him to improve his nature.

Confess: Any tendency to place God on your own level, as though he is subject to the same laws and limitations of creation as you are.

Ask God: To help you perceive his greatness more fully so that you will stop projecting your own feelings and judgments on him.

Imagine for a moment that you live in a world that never changes. In this world civilizations never rise and fall, the weather is constant, children don't grow up, and people never change jobs. In this world, the same old television shows run year after year.

Wouldn't it bore you to death? Without the right kind of change, there would be no growth or development, no hope, nothing whatever to aim for. No one would ever talk about discerning

God's plan for their lives nor would anyone strive to fulfill their God-given potential because there wouldn't even be a word for "potential." We know that to be human is to be subject to change.

As human beings we need constructive change because both we and the world we live in are imperfect. We are not yet everything God intends us to be. But God himself is already perfect, already everything he needs to be: all-powerful, loving, wise, beautiful, and good. Change could not possibly improve him. Furthermore, he is not subject to a changing universe because he exists outside of time and space. He always was and he always will be. This means that the God who loves you will never stop being who he is. His attitude won't change depending on his mood, depending on your mood.

Perhaps you face unwelcome changes right now: the loss of a loved one, a child leaving home, a dwindling paycheck—the future you counted on suddenly in jeopardy. Or maybe you suffer from a mood disorder, up one day and way down the next.

Let the God who is the same yesterday, today, and forever steady your world today. Whatever challenge or change confronts you, let it drive you toward the God who never changes, a God so stable and strong you can lean on him forever.

Friday

PROMISES ASSOCIATED WITH GOD'S NAME

A promise is only as good as the person who makes it. Sometimes young children make promises they cannot keep, like the one about eating all their vegetables if only you will *please* give them a candy bar right now. Lovers promise to stay together in sickness and in health until death parts them. Yet sometimes they stray. Salespeople promise the moon just to close a deal. But when it comes to making a promise and keeping it, God is not like any of his flawed creatures. He is absolutely reliable, completely trustworthy, entirely able to follow through on his word. As the Creator he has infinite resources to accomplish his purposes. Remember that when you think about the following promises from his word in Scripture.

Promises in Scripture

Do you not know?
Have you not heard?
The LORD is the everlasting God,
the Creator of the ends of the earth.
He will not grow tired or weary,
and his understanding no one can fathom.
He gives strength to the weary
and increases the power of the weak. (Isaiah 40:28–29)

So do not fear, for I am with you;
do not be dismayed, for I am your God.
I will strengthen you and help you;
I will uphold you with my righteous right hand. (Isaiah 41:10)

I will not leave you until I have done what I have promised you.
(Genesis 28:15)

Continued Prayer and Praise

Remember that we bear God's image. (Genesis 9:6)

Thank God for his covenant with all living creatures. (Genesis 9:12–17)

Pray that God will turn darkness to light. (Psalm 18:28)

2

THE GOD WHO SEES ME

EL ROI

The Name

An Egyptian slave, Hagar encountered God in the desert and addressed him as *El Roi,* "the God who sees me." Notably, this is the only occurrence of *El Roi* in the Bible.

Hagar's God is the One who numbers the hairs on our heads and who knows our circumstances, past, present, and future. When you pray to *El Roi,* you are praying to the one who knows everything about you.

Key Scripture

She [Hagar] gave this name to the LORD who spoke to her: "You are the God who sees me," for she said, "I have now seen the One who sees me." That is why the well was called Beer Lahai Roi [the "well of the Living One who sees me"]. (Genesis 16:13–14)

Monday

God Reveals His Name

Now Sarai, Abram's wife, had borne him no children. But she had an Egyptian maidservant named Hagar; so she said to Abram, "The LORD has kept me from having children. Go, sleep with my maidservant; perhaps I can build a family through her."

Abram agreed to what Sarai said. So after Abram had been living in Canaan ten years, Sarai his wife took her Egyptian maidservant Hagar and gave her to her husband to be his wife. He slept with Hagar, and she conceived.

When she knew she was pregnant, she began to despise her mistress. Then Sarai said to Abram, "You are responsible for the wrong I am suffering. I put my servant in your arms, and now that she knows she is pregnant, she despises me. May the LORD judge between you and me."

"Your servant is in your hands," Abram said. "Do with her whatever you think best." Then Sarai mistreated Hagar; so she fled from her.

The angel of the LORD found Hagar near a spring in the desert; it was the spring that is beside the road to Shur. And he said, "Hagar, servant of Sarai, where have you come from, and where are you going?"

"I'm running away from my mistress Sarai," she answered.

Then the angel of the LORD told her, "Go back to your mistress and submit to her." The angel added, "I will so increase your descendants that they will be too numerous to count."

The angel of the LORD also said to her:

"You are now with child
  and you will have a son.
You shall name him Ishmael,
  for the LORD has heard of your misery.

He will be a wild donkey of a man;
his hand will be against everyone
and everyone's hand against him,
and he will live in hostility
toward all his brothers."

She gave this name to the LORD who spoke to her: "You are the God who sees me," for she said, "I have now seen the One who sees me." That is why the well was called Beer Lahai Roi ["the well of the Living One who sees me"]; it is still there, between Kadesh and Bered.

So Hagar bore Abram a son, and Abram gave the name Ishmael to the son she had borne. Abram was eighty-six years old when Hagar bore him Ishmael. (Genesis 16:1–16)

Lord, I praise you for you know the whole story. From beginning to end, you see it all. Give me the humility to admit my limitations. For I don't always see the past accurately, my vision of the present is often blurred, and I am blind when it comes to the future. Help me fasten my eyes on you, trusting in your vision for my life and in your watchful care.

Understanding the Name

In the ancient world it was not uncommon for an infertile wife to arrange for a slave girl to sleep with her husband so that the family could have an heir. In fact, Ishmael, the son born to Abraham and Hagar, would have been considered Sarah's legal offspring. Hagar and Ishmael might have fared better had Hagar not forgotten her place the moment she learned of her pregnancy. Still, Sarah's treatment of her seems inexcusable and harsh. In the midst of her difficulties, Hagar learned that *El Roi* (EL raw-EE) was watching over her and that he had a plan to bless her and her son. One of Abraham's grandsons, Esau, married Ishmael's daughter, and it was the Ishmaelite traders (also referred to as Midianite merchants in Genesis

37:26–28), themselves descended from an Egyptian slave, who transported his great-grandson Joseph into slavery in Egypt.

Studying the Name

1. Why do you think the angel of the Lord began his communication with Hagar by questioning her?
2. Describe what Hagar must have been feeling when she fled from Sarah into the desert. Now describe circumstances in your own life that may have produced similar emotions.
3. What images come immediately to mind when you hear the name *El Roi,* "The God who sees me"?
4. How have you experienced God's watchful care?

Tuesday

Praying the Name

The angel of the Lord *found Hagar near a spring in the desert; it was the spring that is beside the road to Shur. And he said, "Hagar, servant of Sarai, where have you come from, and where are you going?"*

"I'm running away from my mistress Sarai," she answered.

Then the angel of the Lord *told her, "Go back to your mistress and submit to her."*

The angel added, "I will so increase your descendants that they will be too numerous to count." . . .

She gave this name to the Lord *who spoke to her: "You are the God who sees me," for she said, "I have now seen the One who sees me." (Genesis 16:7–13)*

Reflect On:	Genesis 16:1–14
Praise God:	For his eye is on the sparrow.
Offer Thanks:	For God's watchful care.
Confess:	Any tendency to accuse God of abandoning you.
Ask God:	To increase your awareness of his presence.

Most mothers find it reassuring to have a baby monitor in an infant's room. I say "most" because I once heard a story about a young mother whose monitor had the opposite effect. A few minutes after tucking her baby in for his midday nap in the upstairs nursery, the woman suddenly heard a loud crash, as though a two-ton gorilla was rampaging in the nursery. Rushing upstairs, her heart beating wildly, she reached her child's room, threw open the door, and saw something she couldn't possibly have imagined—her baby sleeping quietly in his crib. The monitor, it seems, had picked up sounds transmitted by another monitor in a nearby home. So much for technology!

But that is not all. Now there are products on the market that can keep track of dogs, wallets, elderly parents, parolees, and even potential kidnapping victims. My personal favorite is the "Wherify," a wristwatch-like device that can verify someone's exact location in sixty seconds flat.

Useful as these locator devices are, they would have done Hagar little good because no one seemed to care about her and her unborn child enough to monitor her progress in the desert—no one but *El Roi*, that is.

Alone, impoverished, pregnant—there is almost no worse nightmare for a woman. And yet Hagar discovered she wasn't alone. God had seen her predicament with perfect clarity. He knew about the abuse in the past. He pinpointed her exact position in the present. And he saw what the future held for her—a son named Ishmael, descendants too numerous to count. Hagar and her child would live and not die.

No wonder she was willing to return to Abraham's household as the angel of the Lord instructed. No wonder she called God *El Roi* and then exclaimed, "I have now seen the One who sees me."

El Roi, a God so watchful that he is said to note when even the smallest sparrow falls to the ground—this is the God who watches over you today, whether or not you recognize his presence. Aware that you may sometimes find yourself in desolate places, he is always near, helping you find a path through troubles, working out his plans for your future.

Wednesday

Praying the Name

God heard the boy crying, and the angel of God called to Hagar from heaven and said to her, "What is the matter, Hagar? Do not be afraid; God has heard the boy crying as he lies there. Lift the boy up and take him by the hand, for I will make him into a great nation."

Then God opened her eyes and she saw a well of water. So she went and filled the skin with water and gave the boy a drink. (Genesis 21:17–19)

Reflect On: Genesis 21:1–21
Praise God: For faithfully hearing your prayers.
Offer Thanks: For God's timely help.
Confess: Your disbelief despite the evidence of God's past faithfulness.
Ask God: To hear your cries for help.

Ishmael slumped beneath a bush, hoping for relief from the desert sun. He felt feverish, dizzied by the heat. Hagar had watched him drink the last of the water, greedily sucking at the empty skin. His face was flushed, his speech was blurred. It wouldn't be long, she thought, until the boy was past helping. And what of it? She could do nothing for him.

Unable to bear her helplessness in the face of his anguish, she sat down several yards away and began rocking back and forth, wailing out her grief. The angel of the Lord had named him Ishmael, meaning "God hears." But now the name seemed to mock her. Was God deaf, unable to keep his promise? Or cruel? Was he simply unwilling to listen to her cries for help? She would not allow herself to think so.

In the midst of her despair Hagar suddenly heard a voice calling: "Do not be afraid; God has heard the boy crying. Lift him up and take him by the hand, for I will make him into a great nation." Then God opened Hagar's eyes and she saw the thing she dreamed of—a well full of water.

Many years later, the psalmist echoed words that must surely have been on Hagar's mind during her ordeal: "I am worn out calling for help; my throat is parched. My eyes fail, looking for my God" (Psalm 69:3).

The promise God had made to Hagar and Ishmael so many years before stretched itself thin during their time of trial, but never so thin as to break, for God upheld the word he had spoken years before. Remember this when you fail for a time to find God's help or to receive answers to your prayers. Ask *El Roi,* the God who sees you, to open your eyes to his work and to increase your faith even and especially when his promises seem impossible to fulfill.

Thursday

Praying the Name

The Lord looks down from heaven;
he sees all humankind.
From where he sits enthroned he watches
all the inhabitants of the earth—
he who fashions the hearts of them all,
and observes all their deeds. . . .
Truly the eye of the Lord is on those who fear him,
on those who hope in his steadfast love,
to deliver their soul from death,
and to keep them alive in famine. (Psalm 33:13–15, 18–19 NRSV)

Reflect On: Psalm 33:13–22
Praise God: Because he loves to help the poor and the oppressed.
Offer Thanks: For all the ways God has protected you.
Confess: Any self-centeredness and lack of concern for the needy of this world.
Ask God: To grieve your heart with the things that grieve his.

Srey Dara is the pseudonym of a young Cambodian woman who was married at the age of seventeen to a man who lured her into the sex trade by persuading her to move to a distant province and then abandoning her at a brothel. Resisting the pressure exerted by the brothel's owners, Srey cried out in anguish, "O real God, please help!" But threats of torture and beatings finally wore down her resistance.

"Days passed into weeks, then months. One year turned into three years, and I continued to live the nightmare," she confided to a reporter from *Christianity Today*. "I could not go out freely. I lived like a rat afraid to leave its hole. I could go out only at night and then only to work. I kept asking myself, 'How can I get out of here? Will I live here forever?' There was no hope of escape and I was afraid of AIDS. Sometimes I thought about saving money to buy a gun to kill my husband, but I was only given enough money to buy my breakfast.

"I asked, 'Who is the real God? Please come and take me from this hell.' After I asked who the real God is, I had peace in my heart and hope to escape."

Finally, when she had become too sick to work, a monk paid the brothel owners 10,000 Thai baht (over $200 U.S. currency) to release her. Though Srey thanked the "real God" for saving her, she felt dirty and worthless, thinking she deserved to die. And when she searched for her older sister, who had warned her against moving so far from home in the first place, Srey learned that her sister had died. Stunned by the news, Srey wandered aimlessly until she collapsed under a tree. A Christian couple found her and put her in touch with a ministry to victims of the sex trade, where she learned, as she says, "to know the real God—Jesus." As she explains, her life has taken an entirely different turn: "I understand my life has value, and I can live or do anything like other people. . . . May God stop every darkness perpetrated on girls and women."

To Western ears, Srey's story may sound bizarre, her problems a world away. It sounded that way to me until I read a front-page story about a Chinese immigrant who was recently murdered in a city a few miles from my home. Police believe she was lured from China with the promise of a legitimate job and then forced into prostitution.[3] It seems that sex trafficking is big business just about everywhere. With enough money to cater to every kind of appetite, the United States, along with Germany and Italy, has become a top destination for young women who have been enslaved by international sex traffickers.

Today as you pray, cry out to the God from whose eyes nothing is hidden. Ask him to reveal himself as "the real God" to the millions of women and children around the world who are being victimized by the hidden slavery of sex trafficking.

Friday

Promises Associated with God's Name

Even the most watchful parent has to sleep. But Scripture makes it clear God never slumbers, never looks one way while we head off in another, never misses a millisecond of what is happening on earth. It also assures us God is on the lookout for men and women who are totally committed to him. Why? Because he wants to strengthen their hearts as they serve him. If you are feeling weak in the face of life's challenges, the best way to grow strong is to strengthen your commitment to Christ. Decide to obey fully, to follow completely, to keep your eyes fastened on him. Let *El Roi* take pleasure as he watches over you, and you will soon find your heart stronger and your confidence deeper without quite knowing how it happened.

Promises in Scripture

For the eyes of the Lord range throughout the earth to strengthen those whose hearts are fully committed to him. (2 Chronicles 16:9)

He will not let your foot slip—
he who watches over you will not slumber. . . .
The Lord watches over you—
the Lord is your shade at your right hand;
the sun will not harm you by day,
nor the moon by night.
The Lord will keep you from all harm—
he will watch over your life;
the Lord will watch over your coming and going
both now and forevermore. (Psalm 121:3, 5–8)

The eyes of the Lord are everywhere,
keeping watch on the wicked and the good. (Proverbs 15:3)

Continued Prayer and Praise

Remember that your Father sees the hidden good you do and will reward you. (Matthew 6:3–4)

Ask God to help you do what is right in his eyes. (Deuteronomy 12:28)

Pray that God will enable you to see him for who he is. (Matthew 5:8)

3

God Almighty

אֵל שַׁדַּי

El Shadday

The Name

God revealed himself as *El Shadday*, God Almighty, to Abram and told him of the everlasting covenant he was establishing with him and with his descendants. Until the time of Moses, when another divine name was revealed, the patriarchs considered *El Shadday* the covenant name of God. When we pray to *El Shadday*, we invoke the name of the one for whom nothing is impossible.

Key Scripture

When Abram was ninety-nine years old, the LORD appeared to him and said, "I am God Almighty; walk before me and be blameless. I will confirm my covenant between me and you and will greatly increase your numbers." (Genesis 17:1–2)

Monday

God Reveals His Name

When Abram was ninety-nine years old, the Lord appeared to him and said, "I am God Almighty; walk before me and be blameless. I will confirm my covenant between me and you and will greatly increase your numbers."

Abram fell facedown, and God said to him, "As for me, this is my covenant with you: You will be the father of many nations. No longer will you be called Abram; your name will be Abraham, for I have made you a father of many nations. I will make you very fruitful; I will make nations of you and kings will come from you. I will establish my covenant as an everlasting covenant between me and you and your descendants after you for the generations to come, to be your God and the God of your descendants after you. The whole land of Canaan, where you are now an alien, I will give as an everlasting possession to you and your descendants after you and I will be their God." . . .

God also said to Abraham, "As for Sarai your wife, you are no longer to call her Sarai; her name will be Sarah. I will bless her and will surely give you a son by her. I will bless her so that she will be the mother of nations; kings of peoples will come from her."

Abraham fell facedown; he laughed and said to himself, "Will a son be born to a man a hundred years old? Will Sarah bear a child at the age of ninety?" And Abraham said to God, "If only Ishmael might live under your blessing!" (Genesis 17:1–8, 15–18)

Lord, help me to know you as my All-Powerful God, the one who is able to sustain and bless me, to fulfill every promise he makes. Increase my awe of you and of your power so that, like Abraham, I may follow you faithfully, always believing you are enough for me.

Understanding the Name

The Hebrew *El Shadday* (EL shad-DAI), often translated "God Almighty," may literally be translated "God, the Mountain One." Since many of the gods of the ancient Near East were associated with mountains, early translators may have made an educated guess regarding its meaning. Like the mountains themselves, God is seen as strong and unchanging. *El Shadday* reveals God not only as the one who creates and maintains the universe but who initiates and maintains a covenant with his people. *Shadday* occurs thirty-one times in the book of Job and seventeen times in the rest of the Bible. In the New Testament, the Greek term *Pantokrator* is often translated as "Almighty."

Studying the Name

1. Why do you think God revealed his name when speaking of the covenant he made with Abraham and his descendants?
2. Note that in addition to revealing his name, God also changed Abram's and Sarai's names. What do their new names signify? See also Genesis 12:2–3.
3. What was Abraham's response to the promise and the revelation of God's name? How do you think you would have responded if God had revealed himself to you as he did to Abraham?
4. Galatians 3:7 indicates that "those who believe are children of Abraham." What does God's covenant name, *El Shadday,* God Almighty, mean for your life? How have you experienced God's almighty power working on your behalf?

Tuesday

PRAYING THE NAME

When Abram was ninety-nine years old, the LORD appeared to him and said, "I am God Almighty, walk before me and be blameless. I will confirm my covenant between me and you and will greatly increase your numbers. . . . Abraham fell facedown; he laughed and said to himself, "Will a son be born to a man a hundred years old?" (Genesis 17:1–2, 17)

Reflect On: Genesis 17:1–8, 15–17

Praise God: Because no matter how tough life is, no power in heaven or earth can thwart his plan for us as long as we follow him.

Offer Thanks: That God has made an everlasting covenant with us.

Confess: Any doubts about God's ability or desire to help you.

Ask God: For the faith to believe that he can show his strength *in* you and *for* you when you are at your weakest.

Sometimes it's easier to believe in God's power on a grand scale—creating the universe, sustaining it through time, reigning over the centuries—than it is to believe in his power to keep one simple promise. Abraham's life and legacy offer a study in God's promise-keeping ability. But what about promises he makes to us, like the one about helping us in times of temptation? One of the most challenging verses in all of Scripture for many of us to believe is not the one about creation, the virgin birth, or the resurrection. It's the one that says: "And God is faithful; he will not let you be tempted beyond what you can bear. But when you are tempted, he will also provide a way out so that you can stand up under it" (1 Corinthians 10:13).

What does that mean when you're tempted to scream at a perpetually difficult child, to despair when facing a life-altering illness, to sleep with your boyfriend, or to have an affair because your marriage seems so desperately lonely? Doesn't it mean turning, not to yourself to solve the problem (as if you could), but turning in faith to an all-powerful, almighty God, the only one able to help you find the way out? The next time you feel tempted beyond your power to resist, call on the name of *El Shadday*, asking him to help you bear up under it, confident of his ability to sustain and bless you.

Wednesday

Praying the Name

He who dwells in the shelter of the Most High
will rest in the shadow of the Almighty.
I will say of the Lord, *"He is my refuge and my fortress,*
my God, in whom I trust." . . .
"Because he loves me," says the Lord, *"I will rescue him;*
I will protect him, for he acknowledges my name."
(Psalm 91:1–2, 14)

Reflect On: Psalm 91
Praise God: Because he is a refuge from all storms.
Offer Thanks: For God's sheltering care.
Confess: Any habit of worry that keeps you from depending on the Almighty.
Ask God: To increase your trust in him in the days and months to come.

Several years ago I was going through a difficult time. It was an in-between season, a waiting time in which I both longed for change and dreaded its arrival. For more than sixteen years, I had worked for the same company and lived in the same town. I enjoyed my work, but it had become far too predictable. I didn't want to solve the same problems, jump through the same hoops, achieve the same goals year after year. I needed a fresh challenge, a place to develop new skills, an opportunity to broaden my horizons.

But I didn't know exactly what I was looking for. And I was painfully aware that a new job would mean a new city, new friends, a new church, and a new home. Whenever I thought about the future, I drew a blank.

One night I woke up with the thought crystal clear in my head: "You are in the desert right now. You are in the wilderness." Strangely, the words comforted me. I had been so anxious and confused about the future that I wondered whether I was even on God's radar. Now it seemed as if God was assuring me that he knew where I was, even if I didn't. That experience helped pinpoint my location on a spiritual map.

I knew that in the Bible the desert often represented a place of transition and testing. It was where God's people were challenged to obey and to trust God to lead them into the land of promise. I wanted to be patient with the process, to learn what it meant to rest in the shadow of the Almighty, as Psalm 91 puts it. After waking up that night, I felt calmer. It seemed easier to believe that God would help me through my transition. The months that followed proved me right.

I have since found that Psalm 91 is one of those bread-and-butter psalms that I keep coming back to whenever I need to feed on God's Word. Try it for yourself. Read it through once and then call to mind a period in your life in which you experienced God's care and protection. Perhaps it was in the aftermath of a bad business deal, a serious illness, a near accident, a troubled relationship, or a difficult time of transition. Though you may not have known it then, you see now that Almighty God was a refuge in the midst of your personal desert. He sustained you and fed you. He sheltered you in the wilderness. Thank him for his powerful protection. Tell him that you want to make a habit of resting in his shadow. Then read Psalm 91 again, this time as a promise of future protection. This is a powerful psalm to pray before you go to bed each night.

Thursday

Praying the Name

Joseph is a fruitful vine,
a fruitful vine near a spring,
whose branches climb over a wall.
With bitterness archers attacked him;
they shot at him with hostility.
But his bow remained steady . . .
because of the Almighty, who blesses you
with blessings of the heavens above,
blessings of the deep that lies below,
blessings of the breast and womb.
Your father's blessings are greater
than the blessings of the ancient mountains,
than the bounty of the age-old hills.
(Genesis 49:22–26)

Reflect On: Genesis 49:22–26
Praise God: Because it is his nature to bless those who love him.
Offer Thanks: For the way God has persistently blessed your life.
Confess: Any tendency to believe that God would desert you.
Ask God: To help you become a blessing for others.

It all started with a dream of great blessing that Joseph had when he was a young man, the second youngest of twelve brothers. In the dream he was binding sheaves of grain in a field alongside his brothers. Suddenly, Joseph's sheaf stood upright while his brothers bowed down to it. The dream was so vivid that he made the near-fatal mistake of sharing it with his brothers. Offended by the suggestion that they would ever kowtow to Joseph and jealous because their younger brother was their father's favorite, ten of them decided to get rid of him. Most of us know the story well. But it's worth recapping the obstacles Joseph faced:

1. He was kidnapped.
2. He was almost murdered.
3. He was sold into slavery.
4. He was falsely accused of rape.
5. He was thrown into prison.

Imagine what it would be like to suffer just one of these calamities. But despite them all, Joseph kept rising to the top of the heap. Potiphar, his first Egyptian master, quickly put him in charge of his whole household. When Joseph was jailed, the warden gave him responsibility for running the prison. And finally, Pharaoh was so struck by the young man's wisdom and his ability to interpret dreams that he made him governor of all Egypt. Joseph was like a ball that keeps popping back up whenever it's pushed under water. The further it's pushed, the higher it pops. Joseph's resilience in the face of so many obstacles is compelling evidence of the Almighty's power to bless our lives, regardless of who or what stands in the way.

Remember that the next time you're tempted to doubt God's promises. Nothing can prevent *El Shadday,* our Almighty God, from carrying out his plans and pouring out his blessings on those who belong to him. Pain there will be, confusion, struggle, and difficulty, but God can use even these to bless us as long as we trust him.

As you read the passage above from Genesis, capturing Jacob's blessing over his favorite son Joseph, think about all the ways the Almighty is capable of blessing a person, of all the ways he is capable of blessing you.

Friday

PROMISES ASSOCIATED WITH GOD'S NAME

What if God were good but weak? Beautiful but powerless? He might want to bless us but be unable to. Wouldn't this God of good intentions be a bit pathetic? Would any of us fall on our faces before him like Abraham did when God revealed himself as *El Shadday*? Would we even bother to pray to such a God?

Abraham and his family were surrounded by people who believed in such gods—brittle, silent idols made of wood and stone. Fortunately for him and for us, our God is living and powerful, a God who is able to keep every promise he makes. Though God blessed Abraham with specific promises for his life, we share in those promises by virtue of being sons and daughters of Abraham through the gift of faith.

Promises in Scripture

The name of the LORD is a strong tower:
the righteous run to it and are safe. (Proverbs 18:10)

I will make you into a great nation
and I will bless you;
I will make your name great,
and you will be a blessing.
I will bless those who bless you,
and whoever curses you I will curse;
and all peoples on earth
will be blessed through you. (Genesis 12:2–3)

I will surely bless you and make your descendants as numerous as the stars in the sky and as the sand on the seashore. (Genesis 22:17)

Continued Prayer and Praise

Consider whether the Almighty is on your side. (2 Samuel 5:9–10)

Trust in the Almighty. (Psalm 84)

Return to the Almighty, and he will return to you. (Zechariah 1:2–3)

4

The Everlasting God or the Eternal God

El Olam

The Name

El Olam is the Hebrew name for the God who has no beginning and no end, the God for whom a day is like a thousand years and a thousand years are like a day. His plans stand firm forever, plans to give you a future full of hope. When you pray to the Everlasting God, you are praying to the God whose Son is called the Alpha and the Omega. He is the God whose love endures forever.

Key Scripture

After the treaty had been made at Beersheba, Abimelech and Phicol the commander of his forces returned to the land of the Philistines. Abraham planted a tamarisk tree in Beersheba, and there he called upon the name of the LORD, the Eternal God. (Genesis 21:32–33)

Monday

GOD REVEALS HIS NAME

At that time Abimelech and Phicol the commander of his forces said to Abraham, "God is with you in everything you do. Now swear to me here before God that you will not deal falsely with me or my children or my descendants. Show to me and the country where you are living as an alien the same kindness I have shown to you."

Abraham said, "I swear it."

Then Abraham complained to Abimelech about a well of water that Abimelech's servants had seized. But Abimelech said, "I don't know who has done this. You did not tell me, and I heard about it only today."

So Abraham brought sheep and cattle and gave them to Abimelech, and the two men made a treaty. Abraham set apart seven ewe lambs from the flock, and Abimelech asked Abraham, "What is the meaning of these seven ewe lambs you have set apart by themselves?"

He replied, "Accept these seven lambs from my hand as a witness that I dug this well."

So that place was called Beersheba, because the two men swore an oath there.

After the treaty had been made at Beersheba, Abimelech and Phicol the commander of his forces returned to the land of the Philistines. Abraham planted a tamarisk tree in Beersheba, and there he called upon the name of the LORD, the Eternal God. And Abraham stayed in the land of the Philistines for a long time. (Genesis 21:22–34)

Lord, your love and faithfulness endure forever. Help me to live my daily life with the strength that comes from knowing that I am going to live with you forever.

Understanding the Name

Olam is a Hebrew word that occurs more than four hundred times in the Hebrew Scriptures. It is translated as "eternal," "everlasting," "forever," "lasting," "ever," or "ancient." It refers to the fullness of the experience of time or space. The title *El Olam* (EL o-LAM), meaning "Eternal God" or "Everlasting God," appears only four times. The word is applied to God and his laws, promises, covenant, and kingdom.

Studying the Name

1. Abimelech was the leader of the Philistines. What do his words say about the obvious nature of God's faithfulness to Abraham?
2. Beersheba means "well of the oath." Why do you think Abraham planted a tamarisk (a relatively long-lived tree requiring large amounts of water and producing as many as 500,000 seeds per plant) after the two men swore an oath about Abraham's well?
3. What images come to mind when you think of the "Eternal God" or the "Everlasting God"?
4. What might these names imply about the nature of God's promises?

Tuesday

PRAYING THE NAME

For a thousand years in your sight
are like a day that has just gone by,
or like a watch in the night. . . .
The length of our days is seventy years—
or eighty, if we have the strength;
yet their span is but trouble and sorrow,
for they quickly pass, and we fly away. . . .
Teach us to number our days aright,
that we may gain a heart of wisdom. (Psalm 90:4, 10, 12)

Reflect On: Psalm 90
Praise God: For he has no beginning and no end.
Offer Thanks: That God has made your soul immortal.
Confess: Any tendency to live without reference to heaven.
Ask God: To make you grateful for every day that passes.

Jeanne Calment, a French woman, who took up fencing lessons at the age of eighty-five and rode her bike until she was one hundred, lived to be 122 years old. She credited her long life to drinking Port wine, a diet rich in olive oil, and her sense of humor. "I will die laughing," she predicted. In fact, Jeanne had the last laugh when it came to a business deal she made when she was ninety years old. In 1965 a forty-seven-year-old lawyer offered to purchase Jeanne's apartment. He agreed to pay her $500 a month for the rest of her life on the condition that ownership of the apartment would immediately revert to him after her death.

But his gamble, which must have seemed a sure bet, never paid off. Though the lawyer lived to the respectable age of seventy-seven, Jeanne outfoxed him by living a year longer than he did. Over the course of thirty years the lawyer had paid Jeanne a total of $184,000, more than twice the market value of the apartment. To add insult to injury, his heirs were obligated to continue the payments until her death.

When it comes to age, other world record holders have attributed their longevity to "not moping around," "just loving your brother and drinking a glass of red wine," "sipping green tea," and "eating plenty of boiled dandelion greens." Genetics, attitude, diet, the air we breathe—who knows why some people live longer than others? But even 122 years is not much compared to eternity.

Scripture teaches us that wisdom comes, not from living a long life, but from numbering our days aright, which is another way of reminding us that death could come to us anytime, anywhere, at any moment. For those who have faith in the everlasting God, this prospect can help keep us humble and focused, humble because we recognize our limitations and focused because we believe that every day matters. Let it be said of us, not that we died laughing (great as that might be), but that we died loving, trusting our eternal future to the everlasting faithfulness of God.

Wednesday

Praying the Name

Even to your old age and gray hairs
I am he, I am he who will sustain you.
I have made you and I will carry you;
I will sustain you and I will rescue you. (Isaiah 46:4)

Do you not know?
Have you not heard?
The L*ORD is the everlasting God,*
the Creator of the ends of the earth.
He will not grow tired or weary,
and his understanding no one can fathom.
He gives strength to the weary
and increases the power of the weak. (Isaiah 40:28–29)

Reflect On: Isaiah 46:4 and 40:28–31
Praise God: For his eternal vitality.
Offer Thanks: That God promises strength for the weary.
Confess: Any tendency to complain of your aches and pains rather than praying about them.
Ask God: To increase your strength and renew your energy.

Imagine donning an outfit that looks like a cross between a jump-suit and a straightjacket. The material is so stiff around your knees, elbows, ankles, and wrists that it hurts to move your joints. Additional material at the waist makes you feel as though you've gained a tire around your middle. Add gloves and scratched yellow goggles that reduce your sense of touch and sight and you will begin to get an idea of what your body will feel like thirty years hence. At least that's the idea behind The Third Age Suit, a getup worn by mostly thirty-five-year-old and under car designers at Ford Motor Company in an attempt to understand what it feels like to be a senior citizen. Through this method they hope to design more comfortable cars for seniors to drive.

Fortunately the Lord, who made us, has no need to dress up in our skin to understand exactly how aging affects our bodies. This God, who understands what we are going through at every stage of our lives, promises to carry and sustain us even to our old age and gray hairs. He promises to draw from his strength to ease our weakness.

In light of God's faithfulness, it may be that aging is more of a blessing than it seems because the physical decline that accompanies old age can press us toward him, helping us to recognize our limitations, to admit our need. By now any illusion of physical immortality, so easy to believe in when we are young, has been shattered. We begin to perceive our situation more clearly.

Whether you are young or old, take some time to thank God for everything in your body that is working well. Then think about some part of your body or your spirit that needs to be strengthened. Ask God to glorify himself by making you an example of a person who is tangibly strengthened by the Everlasting God, who gives strength to the weary and power to the weak.

Thursday

PRAYING THE NAME

He [God] has also set eternity in the hearts of men. (Ecclesiastes 3:11)

Now this is eternal life: that they may know you, the only true God, and Jesus Christ, whom you have sent. (John 17:3)

Reflect On: Ecclesiastes 3:11 and John 17
Praise God: Who is the Alpha and the Omega, the one who is, who was, and is to come.
Offer Thanks: For the promise of eternal life.
Confess: Any tendency to live as though this world is all there is.
Ask God: To deepen your hope of heaven.

No doubt people will debate whether there is life after death until the world ends. Even those of us who believe in the existence of eternal life aren't in any hurry to verify it through personal experience. The novelist W. Somerset Maugham once said: "Dying is a very dull, dreary affair. And my advice to you is to have nothing to do with it." Winston Churchill, by contrast, seemed prepared for the end when he quipped: "I am ready to meet my Maker. Whether my Maker is prepared for the great ordeal of meeting me is another matter."

Though the debate about immortality still rages, Jesus assures us that there is such a thing as eternal life. One of his most quoted sayings is from John 3:16: "For God so loved the world that he gave his one and only Son, that whoever believes in him shall not perish but have eternal life." The ultimate price for the ultimate prize. The death of God's Son brings us eternal life.

Is it any wonder that the Eternal God wants a people he can love eternally? Is it so hard to fathom that God's love is stronger than death? Is it impossible to believe what can happen to souls created to be wide and deep enough for God to dwell in? No wonder Scripture tells us that the Lord has set eternity in our hearts.

If you believe that Jesus is neither a liar nor a fool, you must believe in the existence of an afterlife. Perhaps the challenge is not only to believe that those who belong to Jesus are destined for heaven but to live in a way that expresses heaven as your deepest longing, your true home.

Friday

PROMISES ASSOCIATED WITH GOD'S NAME

Mercurial, temperamental, erratic, inconsistent, indecisive—we can be thankful that none of these terms apply to the Everlasting God or to his plans for us. Here on earth, we sometimes emphasize how definite our plans are by saying they are "set in concrete." By human standards, that's pretty definite. But even concrete, as indestructible as it seems, can be damaged or destroyed by water, chemicals, fire, or freezing temperatures. Nothing in the universe is as solid as God's plans. Scripture tells us that the purposes of his heart stand firm forever. Because of that, we can be confident that when the created world passes away, Jesus will be there to raise us up if we have put our faith in him.

Promises in Scripture

But the plans of the LORD stand firm forever,
the purposes of his heart through all generations. (Psalm 33:11)

For my Father's will is that everyone who looks to the Son and believes in him shall have eternal life, and I will raise him up at the last day. (John 6:40)

Enter his gates with thanksgiving
and his courts with praise;
give thanks to him and praise his name.
For the LORD is good and his love endures forever
his faithfulness continues through all generations. (Psalm 100:4–5)

Continued Prayer and Praise

Praise the Everlasting God and his Son Jesus. (Revelation 1:4–8)

Thank God for his everlasting love. (Psalm 100)

Praise the Eternal God, who knows our limitations. (Psalm 103:13–18)

Realize that God's promises will never fail us. (Psalm 145:13–14)

5

The Lord Will Provide

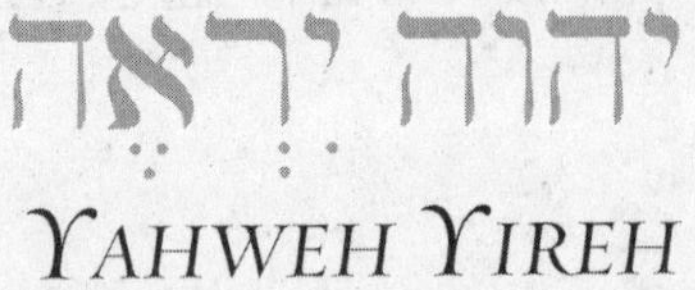

Yahweh Yireh

The Name

The Hebrew word *raah* (RA-ah, from which *yireh* is derived) means "to see." In this case, it is translated as "provide." Since God sees the future as well as the past and the present, he is able to anticipate and provide for what is needed. Interestingly the English word "provision" is made up of two Latin words that mean "to see beforehand." When you pray to *Yahweh Yireh*, you are praying to the God who sees the situation beforehand and is able to provide for your needs.

Key Scripture

Abraham looked up and there in a thicket he saw a ram caught by its horns. He went over and took the ram and sacrificed it as a burnt offering instead of his son. So Abraham called that place The Lord Will Provide. And to this day it is said, "On the mountain of the Lord it will be provided." (Genesis 22:13–14)

Monday

GOD REVEALS HIS NAME

Some time later God tested Abraham. He said to him, "Abraham!"

"Here I am," he replied.

Then God said, "Take your son, your only son, Isaac, whom you love, and go to the region of Moriah. Sacrifice him there as a burnt offering on one of the mountains I will tell you about."

Early the next morning Abraham got up and saddled his donkey. He took with him two of his servants and his son Isaac. When he had cut enough wood for the burnt offering, he set out for the place God had told him about. On the third day Abraham looked up and saw the place in the distance. He said to his servants, "Stay here with the donkey while I and the boy go over there. We will worship and then we will come back to you."

Abraham took the wood for the burnt offering and placed it on his son Isaac, and he himself carried the fire and the knife. As the two of them went on together, Isaac spoke up and said to his father Abraham, "Father?"

"Yes, my son?" Abraham replied.

"The fire and wood are here," Isaac said, "but where is the lamb for the burnt offering?"

Abraham answered, "God himself will provide the lamb for the burnt offering, my son." And the two of them went on together.

When they reached the place God had told him about, Abraham built an altar there and arranged the wood on it. He bound his son Isaac and laid him on the altar, on top of the wood. Then he reached out his hand and took the knife to slay his son. But the angel of the LORD called out to him from heaven, "Abraham! Abraham!"

"Here I am," he replied.

"Do not lay a hand on the boy," he said. "Do not do anything to him. Now I know that you fear God, because you have not withheld from me your son, your only son."

Abraham looked up and there in a thicket he saw a ram caught by its horns. He went over and took the ram and sacrificed it as a burnt offering instead of his son. So Abraham called that place The LORD Will Provide. And to this day it is said, "On the mountain of the LORD it will be provided." (Genesis 22:1–14)

Yahweh Yireh, the Lord who provides for me, thank you for all your blessings—for forgiveness and faith, purpose and hope, food and shelter, family and friends, strength and wisdom, rest and work, laughter and light. Your blessings never come to an end because you are a God of infinite grace. Amen.

Understanding the Name

Moriah, the site of Abraham's thwarted attempt to sacrifice his son, has been traditionally associated with the temple mount in Jerusalem. Today Mount Moriah is occupied by a Muslim shrine called the Dome of the Rock. Jesus, whom John the Baptist called "the Lamb of God," is thought to have been crucified just a quarter mile away from Mount Moriah. It was there that *Yahweh Yireh* (yah-WEH yir-EH) provided the one sacrifice that would make our peace with him.

Studying the Name

1. Imagine that you are Abraham, making the three-day trip toward Moriah to sacrifice your son. What is in your heart?
2. Abraham was determined to obey the command to sacrifice Isaac. Why do you think he told his servants that he and his son would worship and then come back to them? See Hebrews 11:17–19.
3. What is the most difficult sacrifice the Lord has asked you to make? How did you respond?
4. Why do you think God tests people?

5. Compare the scene in which a ram is sacrificed in Isaac's place to this passage from John 1:29: "The next day John [the Baptist] saw Jesus coming toward him and said, 'Look, the Lamb of God, who takes away the sin of the world!'"
6. In what ways has God provided for you?

Tuesday

PRAYING THE NAME

Abraham looked up and there in a thicket he saw a ram caught by its horns. He went over and took the ram and sacrificed it as a burnt offering instead of his son. So Abraham called that place The LORD Will Provide. And to this day it is said, "On the mountain of the LORD it will be provided." (Genesis 22:13–14)

Reflect On: Genesis 22:1–14
Praise God: For his loving provision in your life.
Offer Thanks: For the way God has provided for your spiritual, material, and emotional needs.
Confess: Any tendency to live as though God's grace is cheap.
Ask God: To help you obey him without hesitation or compromise.

A real man, a real boy, walked up the mountain together—the young man bent under the wood for the burnt offering, the father striding behind, carrying the fire and the knife. "But where is the lamb for the sacrifice?" Isaac asked.

"God himself will provide the lamb for the burnt offering, my son," replied Abraham.

We have heard the story before. We know how it ends. But what if we didn't? What if Isaac had been our son, the fulfillment of a promise God had made to us? Could we have traveled for three days to Mount Moriah, the place of sacrifice, dreading the moment and yet walking steadily toward it? Could we have taken the knife in our own hand, willing ourselves to obey the command we did not understand and wished we had not heard?

It is hard to read the story without imagining how Abraham must have felt. Was his hand shaking as he held the knife? Was his mind reeling under the burden of the terrible command he was about to obey? It is not hard to imagine his agony.

But have you ever considered it from God's point of view? Watching the man and his son, did God feel something tearing at his heart, knowing that what he asked but did not require of Abraham—the sacrifice of his only son—he would one day require of himself?

As you read and reflect on the story of how *Yahweh Yireh* provided for Abraham and Isaac, try reading it from God's point of view. Try looking through the eyes of the heavenly Father, who would one day make the costliest of all sacrifices, providing his only Son as the ransom for your soul.

Wednesday

PRAYING THE NAME

He [Abraham] bound his son Isaac and laid him on the altar, on top of the wood. Then he reached out his hand and took the knife to slay his son. But the angel of the LORD *called out to him from heaven, "Abraham! Abraham!"*

"Here I am," he replied.

"Do not lay a hand on the boy," he said. "Do not do anything to him. Now I know that you fear God, because you have not withheld from me your son, your only son." (Genesis 22:9–12)

Reflect On: Genesis 22:9–12
Praise God: Because he is highly exalted, glorious beyond our understanding.
Offer Thanks: That God has pursued a relationship with you.
Confess: Your tendency to shrink back when God asks something difficult.
Ask God: For the grace to make the necessary sacrifice.

This passage captures one of the most dramatic moments in the entire Bible. It's a scene filled with tension. A man is about to slay his only son, not as act of cruelty or rage but out of homage to his God. The story shocks and bewilders. What kind of God would ask a man to do this? What kind of man would obey?

The questions betray our ignorance. Seeing the story through human eyes, we miss the point and fail to see what it means to be God and what it means to be human.

Why would God ask for such a sacrifice? Because he knows there is no other way for us to learn that he is God. When we put something on the altar, sacrificing it to him, we acknowledge two things: that he is God, and that we are not God. This is the worship we need to offer, the worship that will allow us to experience his provision for our lives.

Each of us will be faced with Abraham's dilemma, perhaps many times in our lives. In our case, it won't be a matter of physically placing a child on an altar, but it may mean placing a child in God's hands, forswearing our tendency to be a little god to that child, trying to control her universe and to keep her safe. If not a child, then something else—a relationship, a career, a gift, a dream. Whatever it is, if we offer it to God as Abraham offered his only son, we will begin to know God as *Yahweh Yireh*, the Lord who provides everything we need.

Pray for the grace today to surrender your life again to God. Open your hands as you kneel before him as a symbol of your willingness to give him whatever he asks and to receive whatever you need.

Thursday

PRAYING THE NAME

I swear by myself, declares the LORD, that because you have not withheld your son, your only son, I will surely bless you and make your descendants as numerous as the stars in the sky and as the sand on the seashore. Your descendants will take possession of the cities of their enemies, and through your offspring all nations on earth will be blessed, because you have obeyed me. (Genesis 22:16–18)

Reflect On:	Genesis 22:15–18
Praise God:	Because he delights in blessing his people.
Offer Thanks:	For the blessings you have received because of Abraham's obedience.
Confess:	Any tendency to attribute God's blessings to yourself.
Ask God:	To help you experience the connection between obedience and blessing.

Abraham was one of the Bible's most successful men, blessed with a long life, many children, great personal wealth, and a profound spiritual legacy. What was the simple secret of his success? Obedience. Because of it, Abraham didn't need a bull market in order to prosper. He only needed to do God's will. His obedience was the capital he invested, the principal that yielded an enormous return.

Without obedience we will never experience the provision God intends for us. Alexander MacClaren, a nineteenth-century Scottish preacher, reminds us that God's provision is not automatic:

> If we wish to have our outward needs supplied, our outward weaknesses strengthened, power and energy sufficient for duty, wisdom for perplexity, a share in the Sacrifice which takes away the sins of the world, we receive them all on the

> condition that we are found in the place where all God's provision is treasured. If a man chooses to sit outside the baker's shop, he may starve on its threshold. . . . And if we will not ascend to the hill of the Lord and stand in his holy place by simple faith, and by true communion of heart and life, God's amplest provision is nought to us; and we are empty in the midst of affluence.

If you have been "sitting outside the baker's shop," hungry for God's blessing, ask him to help you to move inside by giving you the grace to obey even the smallest command. Before long your small steps of obedience will lead to larger ones and then your steady habit of obedience will lead to deepened faith, enabling you to experience God as Abraham did, as *Yahweh Yireh.*

Friday

PROMISES ASSOCIATED WITH GOD'S NAME

Scripture is full of the promises of God, and when we respond to him faithfully, nothing can prevent their fulfillment. That holds true regardless of circumstances. Think for a moment about Abraham's circumstances. God had promised his descendants would be as numerous as the stars in the sky and the sand on the seashore. But how could that promise be fulfilled if the first star, the first grain of sand—if Isaac himself—were destroyed? Ironically, the promise was fulfilled precisely *because* Abraham was willing to act in a way that seemed contrary to its fulfillment. Had Abraham refused to obey God, he might well have forfeited the incredible blessings that followed.

True, the specific promises God made to Abraham do not apply to us in exactly the way they did to him. But the principle is the same. When it comes to the things God *has* promised us—wisdom, strength for our trials, a way out of temptation, and fullness of life—our obedience is key. No matter what the circumstances, we need to realize there is no limit to God's power to do what he says—if we believe and obey.

Promises in Scripture

For in the land the L*ORD your God is giving you to possess as your inheritance, he will richly bless you, if only you fully obey the* L*ORD your God and are careful to follow all these commands I am giving you today. (Deuteronomy 15:4–5)*

So, if you think you are standing firm, be careful that you don't fall! No temptation has seized you except what is common to man. And God is faithful; he will not let you be tempted beyond what you can bear. But when you are tempted, he will also provide a way out so that you can stand up under it. (1 Corinthians 10:12–13)

Continued Prayer and Praise

Reflect on God's provision for your life. (Matthew 6:28–30)

Pray for the grace to reflect God's generosity by generously providing for others. (1 Timothy 6:17–19)

6

LORD

יהוה

YAHWEH

The Name

The name *Yahweh* (yah-WEH) occurs more than 6,800 times in the Old Testament. It appears in every book but Esther, Ecclesiastes, and the Song of Songs. As the sacred, personal name of Israel's God, it was eventually spoken aloud only by priests worshiping in the Jerusalem temple. After the destruction of the temple in A.D. 70, the name was not pronounced. *Adonay* was substituted for *Yahweh* whenever it appeared in the biblical text. Because of this, the correct pronunciation of this name was eventually lost. English editions of the Bible usually translate *Adonay* as "Lord" and *Yahweh* as "LORD." *Yahweh* is the name that is most closely linked to God's redeeming acts in the history of his chosen people. We know God because of what he has done. When you pray to *Yahweh,* remember that he is the same God who draws near to save you from the tyranny of sin just as he saved his people from tyrannical slavery in Egypt.

Key Scripture

God said to Moses, "I AM WHO I AM. This is what you are to say to the Israelites: 'I AM has sent me to you.'"

God also said to Moses, "Say to the Israelites, 'The LORD [Yahweh], the God of your fathers—the God of Abraham, the God of Isaac and the God of Jacob—has sent me to you.' This is my name forever, the name by which I am to be remembered from generation to generation." (Exodus 3:14–15)

Monday

GOD REVEALS HIS NAME

Now Moses was tending the flock of Jethro his father-in-law, the priest of Midian, and he led the flock to the far side of the desert and came to Horeb, the mountain of God. There the angel of the LORD appeared to him in flames of fire from within a bush. Moses saw that though the bush was on fire it did not burn up. So Moses thought, "I will go over and see this strange sight—why the bush does not burn up." . . .

Moses hid his face, because he was afraid to look at God.

The LORD said, "I have indeed seen the misery of my people in Egypt. I have heard them crying out because of their slave drivers, and I am concerned about their suffering. So I have come down to rescue them. . . . I am sending you to Pharaoh to bring my people the Israelites out of Egypt."

But Moses said to God, "Who am I, that I should go to Pharaoh and bring the Israelites out of Egypt?"

And God said, "I will be with you. And this will be the sign to you that it is I who have sent you: When you have brought the people out of Egypt, you will worship God on this mountain."

Moses said to God, "Suppose I go to the Israelites and say to them, 'The God of your fathers has sent me to you,' and they ask me, 'What is his name?' Then what shall I tell them?"

God said to Moses, "I AM WHO I AM. This is what you are to say to the Israelites: 'I AM has sent me to you.'"

God also said to Moses, "Say to the Israelites, 'The LORD, the God of your fathers—the God of Abraham, the God of Isaac and the God of Jacob—has sent me to you.' This is my name forever, the name by which I am to be remembered from generation to generation.

"Go, assemble the elders of Israel and say to them, 'The LORD, the God of your fathers—the God of Abraham, Isaac and Jacob—

appeared to me and said: I have watched over you and have seen what has been done to you in Egypt. And I have promised to bring you up out of your misery in Egypt into the land of the Canaanites, Hittites, Amorites, Perizzites, Hivites and Jebusites—a land flowing with milk and honey.'

"The elders of Israel will listen to you. Then you and the elders are to go to the king of Egypt and say to him, 'The LORD, the God of the Hebrews, has met with us. Let us take a three-day journey into the desert to offer sacrifices to the LORD our God.' But I know that the king of Egypt will not let you go unless a mighty hand compels him. So I will stretch out my hand and strike the Egyptians with all the wonders that I will perform among them. After that, he will let you go." (Exodus 3:1–3, 6–8, 10–20)

I will sing to you, Yahweh, for you are highly exalted. The horse and its rider you have hurled into the sea. Yahweh, you are my strength and my song; you have become my salvation. You are my God, and I will praise you. Amen.

Understanding the Name

Afraid of profaning this covenant name of God, various rabbinical writers spoke of it as "The Name," "The Great and Terrible Name," "The Unutterable Name," "The Ineffable Name," "The Holy Name," and "The Distinguished Name." Also known as the Tetragrammaton, because it is formed by the four Hebrew consonants YHWH (JHVH in German), it was first rendered *Jehovah* in the Middle Ages and enshrined as such in the King James Version of the Bible (Exodus 6:3; Psalm 83:18; Isaiah 12:2; 26:4). This mispronunciation arose when in the tenth-century Jewish scholars began supplying vowels to Hebrew words, which had formerly been written without them. Since *Adonay* was always substituted for *Yahweh* (pronounced yah-WEH, as scholars now think) in the biblical text, the Hebrew vowels for *Adonay* were inserted into the four letters of the Tetragrammaton: YaHoWaH.

Unfortunately, the translation "LORD," which is a title rather than a name, obscures the personal nature of this name for God. Though the meaning of *Yahweh* is disputed, the mysterious self-description in Exodus 3:14, "I AM WHO I AM," may convey the sense not only that God is self-existent but that he is always present with his people. *Yahweh* is not a God who is remote or aloof but One who is always near, intervening in history on behalf of his people. The knowledge of God's proper name implies a covenant relationship. God's covenant name is closely associated with his saving acts in Exodus. The name *Yahweh* evokes images of God's saving power in the lives of his people.

Studying the Name

1. What does this passage reveal about what was in the heart of God in regard to his people?
2. What was the catalyst for God's action?
3. Moses' reluctance is not hard to understand. Describe a time when you were similarly reluctant to do something you thought God was calling you to do.
4. Why do you think Moses asked God to reveal his name?

Tuesday

Praying the Name

And God said, "I will be with you. And this will be the sign to you that it is I who have sent you: When you have brought the people out of Egypt, you will worship God on this mountain."

God said to Moses, "I AM WHO I AM. This is what you are to say to the Israelites: 'I AM has sent me to you.'"

God also said to Moses, "Say to the Israelites, 'The LORD [Yahweh], the God of your fathers—the God of Abraham, the God of Isaac and the God of Jacob—has sent me to you.' This is my name forever, the name by which I am to be remembered from generation to generation." (Exodus 3:12–15)

I am the LORD [Yahweh] your God, who brought you out of the land of Egypt, out of the land of slavery. You shall have no other gods before me. (Exodus 20:2–3)

Reflect On: Exodus 3:12–15; 20:2
Praise God: For revealing himself through powerful acts of deliverance.
Offer Thanks: That God has freed you from every form of bondage.
Confess: Any tendency to forget what God has done for you.
Ask God: To help you remember his saving acts in your life.

I AM WHO I AM

What do these mysterious words mean? Was Moses as bewildered as we are by God's self-disclosure? Or did he realize that God was assuring him he would always be present to his people—listening for their cries, answering their prayers, showing his power on their behalf, responding faithfully even when they acted faithlessly?

Yahweh. The name couldn't have clarified things. It may have sounded odd at first, like a name you warm to over time, much as an infant warms to the word Mama, gradually equating her with safety, food, and help.

To the Egyptians the name *Yahweh* would have been a terror—a name to forget because it conjured plagues, darkness, defeat, and death. But to Moses and the Israelites *Yahweh* would forever mean deliverance, freedom, promise, and power. God's people could not invoke his name without remembering what it was like to walk through the parted waters of the Red Sea, to gather manna in the wilderness, to receive the commandments on Sinai.

The amazing events of Exodus defined who *Yahweh* was in extraordinary detail. *Yahweh*—Israel's faithful, wonder-working God, the One who out of pity and love reached into human history to untie the bonds of an enslaved people—that was the name by which this God wanted to be forever known.

Today, when you bow before *Yahweh*, thank him for the deliverance he has wrought in your own life. Acknowledge your need for him. Recommit yourself to living by the ten commandments he gave, the law that enabled his people to live in his presence, confident of his care.

Wednesday

Praying the Name

Praise the Lord [Yahweh], O my soul;
all my inmost being, praise his holy name.
Praise the Lord [Yahweh], O my soul,
and forget not all his benefits—
who forgives all your sins
and heals all your diseases,
who redeems your life from the pit
and crowns you with love and compassion,
who satisfies your desires with good things
so that your youth is renewed like the eagle's.
The Lord [Yahweh] works righteousness
and justice for all the oppressed.
He made known his ways to Moses,
his deeds to the people of Israel:
The Lord [Yahweh] is compassionate and gracious,
slow to anger, abounding in love.
He will not always accuse,
nor will he harbor his anger forever;
he does not treat us as our sins deserve
or repay us according to our iniquities.
For as high as the heavens are above the earth
so great is his love for those who fear him;
as far as the east is from the west,
so far has he removed our transgressions from us.
As a father has compassion on his children,
so the Lord [Yahweh] has compassion on those
who fear him. (Psalm 103:1–13)

Reflect On:	Psalm 103
Praise God:	Because his goodness never fails.
Offer Thanks:	For God's continued forgiveness.
Confess:	Any tendency to impute motives to God unworthy of his character.
Ask God:	To break any false images of him that you may have developed.

My eight-year-old daughter is an artist. Her drawings of cats, horses, dinosaurs, dragons, lions, tigers, alligators, elephants, and assorted monsters look so real that it isn't hard imagining them jumping right off the page and rollicking around the house. She has an artist's eye for detail, which is one reason why her pictures look so real. One night after I'd returned from a too-lengthy business trip, she threw her arms around me, exclaiming: "You have the best mommy face in the whole world! I like the way it looks. It goes great with your hair and the glasses work pretty well too!" It wasn't only her artist eyes noting all the details. Her picture of me was filtered through eyes of love.

I wish I could tell you that my daughter's assessment is always so flattering. Her perception changes dramatically whenever I press her to do something she'd really rather not, holding her to a higher standard than she has for herself. Maybe that's why most of us have difficulty realizing how much God loves us. We conclude he's angry or uncaring because he doesn't answer every prayer in the way we want. Like my eight-year-old, we lack the spiritual maturity to realize that God is acting like a loving father when he uses hardships to discipline us (Proverbs 3:12).

It's so easy to develop an image of God that is the opposite from the loving and compassionate God described in Psalm 103. One way to counter that tendency is to paint a picture in your mind of the God the psalmist describes, using these words to shape the image of him you hold in your heart:

- Forgiving
- Healing
- Redeeming
- Compassionate
- Delighting to bless you
- Working on behalf of the oppressed
- Slow to anger
- Gracious
- Loving

Take time today to praise *Yahweh*, using these descriptive images as you bow down before him.

Thursday

Praying the Name

An angel of the Lord appeared to him in a dream and said, "Joseph son of David, do not be afraid to take Mary home as your wife, because what is conceived in her is from the Holy Spirit. She will give birth to a son, and you are to give him the name Jesus, because he will save his people from their sins." (Matthew 1:20–21)

Jesus replied [to Jews who accused him of being demon-possessed], "If I glorify myself, my glory means nothing. My Father, whom you claim as your God, is the one who glorifies me. Though you do not know him, I know him. If I said I did not, I would be a liar like you, but I do know him and keep his word. Your father Abraham rejoiced at the thought of seeing my day; he saw it and was glad."

"You are not yet fifty years old," the Jews said to him, "and you have seen Abraham!"

"I tell you the truth," Jesus answered, "before Abraham was born, I am!" At this, they picked up stones to stone him, but Jesus hid himself, slipping away from the temple grounds. (John 8:54–59)

Reflect On: Matthew 1:20–21; John 8:54–59
Praise God: For foreseeing your need for a Savior.
Offer Thanks: For his delivering power.
Confess: Your continuing need for God's forgiveness.
Ask God: For a living understanding of what Jesus has done for you.

Christmas means lighted trees, presents, parties, and pageants full of pint-size shepherds and pudgy-faced angels proclaiming the birth of the Lord. We crane our necks, hoping our children won't botch their lines, smiling as they charmingly reenact the old story. We're full of Christmas cheer, happy to celebrate again with friends and family. It's a wonderful season. But in all our Christmas frenzy, we often forget to wonder—

- about what it was like for a poor man to find shelter for his pregnant wife
- about the sound of the woman's cries as she gave birth in a dirty stable
- about the audacity of God entrusting his own Son to two people who seemed hardly able to care for themselves

Most of us also fail to wonder about the infant's name, given by an angel, a name linked to the holiest name in all of Scripture. For "Jesus," a form of "Joshua," means only this: *Yahweh Saves.* This time *Yahweh* would be present with his people not in the form of a burning bush but in the shape of a small child who later would provoke people to violence precisely because he echoed God's self-revelation to Moses in the wilderness: "I tell you the truth, before Abraham was born, *I am!*"

Though today may not be Christmas Day, it's a perfect day to bow down before our faithful, covenant-keeping God, praising him for the gift of his only Son, Jesus, the One who reminds us still that *Yahweh Saves.*

Friday

PROMISES ASSOCIATED WITH GOD'S NAME

My father had a name for people who make grandiose statements or offer promises they can't keep. He called them blowhards. In truth, a promise is only as good as the person who makes it. What good is a commitment of undying love from an unfaithful wife, or a twenty-year warranty from a roofer who's about to go bankrupt, or a promissory note from a scoundrel? Fortunately, God doesn't need to exaggerate his abilities. He never makes a promise he cannot keep. If you live in a way that respects God's commandments, you will find that the name of the Lord can always be relied upon, no matter what threatens you.

Promises in Scripture

The LORD [Yahweh] will be your confidence
and will keep your foot from being snared. (Proverbs 3:26)

The name of the LORD [Yahweh] is a strong tower;
the righteous run to it and are safe. (Proverbs 18:10)

The LORD [Yahweh] will establish you as his holy people, as he promised you on oath, if you keep the commands of the LORD [Yahweh] your God and walk in his ways. . . . The LORD [Yahweh] will open the heavens, the storehouse of his bounty, to send rain on your land in season and to bless all the work of your hands. (Deuteronomy 28:9, 12)

Continued Prayer and Praise

Meditate on God's self-description. (Exodus 34:4–7)

Pray this benediction, which includes the threefold repetition of the name *Yahweh*. (Numbers 6:24–27)

Thank *Yahweh* for surrounding you with unfailing love. (Psalm 32:10)

Ask God to deliver you from fear. (Psalm 34:4–5)

Remember that *Yahweh* is close to the brokenhearted. (Psalm 34:18)

Wait for the Lord. (Psalm 37:34–40)

7

LORD, MASTER

ADONAY

The Name

Adonay is a Hebrew word meaning "Lord," a name that implies relationship: God is Lord, and we are his servants. As a word referring to God it appears more than three hundred times in the Hebrew Scriptures. As you pray to *Adonay*, tell him you want to surrender every aspect of your life to him. Pray for the grace to become the kind of servant who is quick to do God's will. Remember, too, that the Lord is the only one who can empower you to fulfill his purpose for your life. In fact, it is in knowing him as your Lord that you will discover a true sense of purpose. The New Testament depicts Jesus as both Lord and Servant. In this latter role he exemplifies what our relationship to *Adonay* is to be.

Key Scripture

You are my Lord; I have no good besides you. (Psalm 16:2 NASB)

Monday

GOD REVEALS HIS NAME

Moses answered, "What if they do not believe me or listen to me and say, 'The LORD [*Yahweh*] did not appear to you'?"

Then the LORD [*Yahweh*] said to him, "What is that in your hand?"

"A staff," he replied.

The LORD [*Yahweh*] said, "Throw it on the ground."

Moses threw it on the ground and it became a snake, and he ran from it. Then the LORD [*Yahweh*] said to him, "Reach out your hand and take it by the tail." So Moses reached out and took hold of the snake and it turned back into a staff in his hand. "This," said the LORD [*Yahweh*], "is so that they may believe that the LORD [*Yahweh*], the God of their fathers—the God of Abraham, the God of Isaac and the God of Jacob—has appeared to you."...

Moses said to the LORD [*Yahweh*], "O Lord [*Adonay*], I have never been eloquent, neither in the past nor since you have spoken to your servant. I am slow of speech and tongue."

The LORD [*Yahweh*] said to him, "Who gave man his mouth? Who makes him deaf or mute? Who gives him sight or makes him blind? Is it not I, the LORD [*Yahweh*]? Now go; I will help you speak and will teach you what to say."

But Moses said, "O Lord [*Adonay*], please send someone else to do it."

Then the LORD's [*Yahweh's*] anger burned against Moses and he said, "What about your brother, Aaron the Levite? I know he can speak well. He is already on his way to meet you, and his heart will be glad when he sees you. You shall speak to him and put words in his mouth; I will help both of you speak and will teach you what to do." (Exodus 4:1–5,10–15)

Lord, forgive me for the times that I have only paid lip service to your lordship in my life. I have prayed one thing and done another. Help me as of this moment to experience the joy of serving you, living with the knowledge that you are my Adonay, my Lord and God. Amen.

Understanding the Name

Adon is a Hebrew word that means "lord" in the sense of an owner, master, or superior. It is frequently used as a term of respect and always refers to people. *Adonay* (a-do-NAI) is the plural form of *adon* and always refers to God as Lord or Master. In the Old Testament it is rendered as "Lord" (distinct from "LORD," the rendering for the Hebrew name *Yahweh*). When *Adonay* and *Yahweh* appear together, the NIV renders the name as "Sovereign LORD," while older translations of the Bible render it "Lord God." *Adonay* is first used in Genesis 15:2. In the New Testament, the Greek word most often translated "Lord" is *Kyrios*.

Studying the Name

1. How is the lordship of God displayed in Exodus 4? (Note that Pharaoh's headdress included a metal cobra, symbolizing his sovereignty.)
2. Why was the Lord angry with Moses?
3. Notice that Moses expressed reluctance to doing God's will at the same time he was addressing him as "Lord." Have you ever done the same? What held you back from doing what the Lord was asking?

Tuesday

PRAYING THE NAME

Suppose one of you had a servant plowing or looking after the sheep. Would he say to the servant when he comes in from the field, "Come along now and sit down to eat"? Would he not rather say, "Prepare my supper, get yourself ready and wait on me while I eat and drink; after that you may eat and drink"? (Luke 17:7–8)

Reflect On:	Luke 17:7–10
Praise God:	Because his greatness compels our service.
Offer Thanks:	For the chance to be used by the Lord.
Confess:	Any disdain for the role of servant.
Ask God:	To give you a greater vision of what it means to be his servant.

Recently my daughters and I took a weeklong cruise aboard a ship with a crew made up of people from all over the world. Though the ship was beautiful, I was even more impressed by people who served us. I had never experienced anything like it. Young people from Croatia, the Philippines, Romania, and South Africa couldn't do enough for us.

Why are there so few Americans among the crew? I wondered. It seemed like an ideal job for a young person who wanted to bank most of his salary and meet lots of interesting people at the same time. But then I remembered the grueling schedule and the menial jobs. Crew members cooked, mopped floors, waited tables, entertained children, and cleaned staterooms seven days a week for six months straight before getting a three-month breather. And each member of the crew seemed dedicated to serving us with a genuine smile. *Would many Americans know how to deliver such an extreme level of service? Would they even want to? Would I want to?* I wondered.

"Servant" is not a particularly popular word in our culture. It sounds demeaning, belittling, hardly something we should aspire to. Such an attitude can make it hard for us to understand our position as servants of the Lord. Perhaps that's why we so often get things reversed, treating God as though he were some kind of celestial butler who should use his divine power to further our plans.

With that kind of attitude underlying our prayers, it is a wonder the Lord answers so many of them. Perhaps it is time to repent and ask God to help us to give him the kind of perfect service that Jesus himself did. Let us bow before the Lord today, asking for only one thing—the grace to glorify him.

Wednesday

PRAYING THE NAME

I said to the LORD, "You are my Lord;
apart from you I have no good thing." (Psalm 16:2)

Whom have I in heaven but you?
And earth has nothing I desire besides you.
My flesh and my heart may fail,
but God is the strength of my heart
and my portion forever. (Psalm 73:25–26)

Reflect On: Psalm 16:2; 73:25–26
Praise God: For he is the source of your life.
Offer Thanks: For all the good things God has given you. (Call specific blessings to mind.)
Confess: Any tendency to withhold certain areas of your life from the Lord.
Ask God: To help you see the connection between his lordship and his blessing.

Imagine that you have inherited a large box filled with diamonds. Along with the box you've also inherited a million different keys, with no indication of which one will open the box. According to the rules of the inheritance you are allowed to try one new key each day until you discover the one key that works. So you start with the most elegant-looking one in the collection. Day after day, you try one key after another, but nothing works. Finally on the one-millionth day, you try the smallest, most corroded key of the bunch, and, of course, it works. Suddenly you are a multimillionaire, rich enough to fulfill your heart's desires. There is just one problem. To use every key, you would have to live to be at least 2,740 years old!

Now consider the story from a different angle. Instead of starting with the most impressive key, let's say you decide to approach the problem counterintuitively by starting with the least attractive key. Bingo! It works. You have instant access to an enormous fortune, more than enough to support you for the rest of your life.

The point of this fanciful story is this: If we want to find the one key to everything good in life, we will need to approach the problem counterintuitively. Instead of operating by instinct, we will operate by faith. Instead of striving to do what we want when we want, we will strive to do what God wants when he wants. As we do, we will begin to understand that his lordship will not diminish or impoverish us but that it will bless us in surprising ways. Astonished by all the good he does in and through us, we will be able to echo the psalmist's praise: "You are my Lord; apart from you I have no good thing."

Don't wait until tomorrow to test out this principle. Tell the Lord you're ready to serve him today. Ask him for opportunities to express your love and your faith. And don't be surprised by the lightning speed with which he answers your prayer.

Thursday

Praying the Name

Don't be afraid of them. Remember the Lord, who is great and awesome, and fight for your brothers, your sons and your daughters, your wives and your homes. (Nehemiah 4:14)

Reflect On: Nehemiah 4:7–18
Praise God: For he is more powerful than our most powerful enemies.
Offer Thanks: That your powerful Lord uses his power on your behalf.
Confess: Any tendency to live by fear and not faith.
Ask God: To help you fight for your marriage, your children, and your home.

Nehemiah helped rebuild Jerusalem more than a hundred years after it had been destroyed by the Babylonians. He began by reminding a demoralized people, not of who they were, but of who God is—"the Lord, who is great and awesome." Having thus rallied them, he succeeded in rebuilding Jerusalem's defensive walls in only fifty-two days, despite significant resistance from outside enemies.

Thousands of years later, we still face forces intent on destroying us—enemies that eat away at faith, that corrode relationships, that destroy families. Some of us are bone weary from the struggle, about to give up on the spouse who seems so distant, the child who has wandered away from God, the job we can't seem to succeed at, or the prayer that has gone so long unanswered. If that describes your spiritual state, let the words of Nehemiah sink into the raw places of your heart where disappointment lodges: "Remember the

Lord, who is great and awesome." Now is not the time to give up or give in. Remember whose servant you are. Fight in his strength for your children, your marriage, your church. Do whatever it takes for however long it takes, knowing the Lord is with you.

Friday

PROMISES ASSOCIATED WITH GOD'S NAME

Unlike the unprincipled political or business leader who uses people up and then discards them, God never fails to sustain us. Knowing that the Lord we serve is also the Lord who loves us, we need not fear that he will take advantage of us or that he will ask us to do something we cannot possibly do. Realizing who the Lord is will enable us to stop worrying about who we are or what we lack so that we can abandon our lives to him, confident we can do whatever he asks through the grace he supplies.

Promises in Scripture

Surely God is my help;
the Lord is the one who sustains me. (Psalm 54:4)

One thing God has spoken,
two things have I heard:
that you, O God, are strong,
and that you, O Lord, are loving. (Psalm 62:11–12)

But you, O Lord, are a compassionate and gracious God,
slow to anger, abounding in love and faithfulness. (Psalm 86:15)

Continued Prayer and Praise

Worship the Lord for his greatness. (Isaiah 6:1–8)

Ask the Lord's forgiveness for yourself and for God's people. (Daniel 9:17–19)

Thank the Lord for his love. (Psalm 136:3)

Pray for the grace to become a servant like Jesus. (Philippians 2:5–11)

8

The Lord Who Heals

Yahweh Rophe

The Name

The Hebrew word *rophe* means "heal, "cure," "restore," or "make whole." Shortly after his people left Israel for the Promised Land, God revealed himself as *Yahweh Rophe,* "the LORD who heals." The Hebrew Scriptures indicate that God is the source of all healing. As you pray to *Yahweh Rophe*, ask him to search your heart. Take time to let him show you what it contains. If he uncovers any sin, ask for his forgiveness and then pray for healing. The New Testament reveals Jesus as the Great Physician, the healer of body and soul, whose miracles point to the kingdom of God.

Key Scripture

If you diligently heed the voice of the LORD your God and do what is right in His sight, give ear to His commandments and keep all His statues, I will put none of the diseases on you which I have brought on the Egyptians. For I *am* the LORD who heals you. (Exodus 15:26 NKJV)

Monday

God Reveals His Name

Then Miriam the prophetess, the sister of Aaron, took the timbrel in her hand; and all the women went out after her with timbrels and with dances. And Miriam answered them:

"Sing to the Lord,
For He has triumphed gloriously!
The Horse and its rider
He has thrown into the sea!"

So Moses brought Israel from the Red Sea; then they went out into the Wilderness of Shur. And they went three days in the wilderness and found no water. Now when they came to Marah, they could not drink the waters of Marah, for they *were* bitter. Therefore the name of it was called Marah [meaning bitter]. And the people complained against Moses, saying, "What shall we drink?" So he cried out to the Lord and the Lord showed him a tree. When he cast *it* into the waters, the waters were made sweet.

There He made a statute and an ordinance for them, and there He tested them, and said, "If you diligently heed the voice of the Lord your God and do what is right in His sight, give ear to His commandments and keep all His statutes, I will put none of the diseases on you which I have brought on the Egyptians. For I *am* the Lord who heals you." (Exodus 15:20–27 NKJV)

Yahweh Rophe, I bow before you today to acknowledge that you are not only my Creator but the Lord who heals me. Please heal me today, body and soul, and do the same for my loved ones. I pray that you will heal whatever is bitter in our lives, transforming us in ways that glorify you. Amen.

Understanding the Name

The verb from which *Rophe* is derived occurs sixty-seven times in the Old Testament. Though it often refers to physical healing, it usually has a larger meaning as well, involving the entire person. Rather than merely healing the body, *Yahweh Rophe* (yah-WEH ro-FEH) heals the mind and soul as well. This Hebrew verb is also used in other ways—for example, God "heals" water, land, and nations, and he "repairs" an altar. Significantly, God also heals sin and apostasy. The Hebrew Scriptures, in fact, link sickness and sin by presenting sin as the cause of illness just as it is the cause of death. In the New Testament, the corresponding Greek word is *iaomai* and it can refer to deliverance from death, demons, sickness, and sin.

Jesus, the great healer, clearly indicated that sickness is not necessarily caused by sin on the part of the person who is ill. Rather, it can result from living in a sinful, fallen world.

Studying the Name

1. In Exodus 15, how did circumstances influence the people's attitude toward God? Describe times in your own life when your circumstances have caused your attitude toward God to fluctuate.
2. How did Moses react to the circumstances? What does his example teach about how we should respond to difficult circumstances?
3. God tested the Israelites with adverse circumstances, thus uncovering what was in their hearts. Describe ways in which you have experienced God testing you. How did you respond?
4. What does this passage say about God's control over sickness and health?

Tuesday

PRAYING THE NAME

If you diligently heed the voice of the LORD your God and do what is right in His sight, give ear to His commandments and keep all His statutes, I will put none of the diseases on you which I have brought on the Egyptians. For I am the LORD who heals you. (Exodus 15:26 NKJV)

Anyone the man with a discharge touches without rinsing his hands with water must wash his clothes and bathe with water, and he will be unclean till evening. (Leviticus 15:11)

Reflect On: Exodus 15:22–26
Praise God: For his great wisdom.
Offer Thanks: That his laws are designed not to harm us but to protect us.
Confess: Any sin that has entered your life through breaking God's commandments.
Ask God: To help you see the link between obedience and health, physical and spiritual.

Ancient medical knowledge was limited not only by the lack of scientific method but also by the widespread worship of idols and the belief in magic. Disease was often blamed on the presence of evil spirits, who could only be vanquished by magical potions and powerful incantations. Egyptian papyri dating to 1552 B.C. list medical remedies containing a strange array of ingredients, including "lizards' blood, swine's teeth, putrid meat, stinking fat, moisture from pigs' ears, milk, goose grease, asses' hoofs, animal fats from various sources, excreta from animals, including human beings, donkeys, antelopes, dogs, cats, and even flies." Clearly this was a case of the cure being worse than the cold.

Rather than relying on a witches' brew of potions to heal them, the Israelites were to obey God's commandments and statutes, some of which contained instructions that foreshadow modern medical discoveries. For instance, people were to wash their bodies and their clothes if they came into contact with a disease, a bodily discharge, or a corpse. This hardly sounds like rocket science unless you realize that as recently as 150 years ago, it was considered ridiculous for a surgeon to have to wash his hands prior to operating on a patient. The Israelites also practiced isolation and quarantine and followed dietary laws that prevented the spread of disease.

One of the ways God lived up to the self-disclosed name *Yahweh Rophe* was in providing his people with instructions that prevented them from becoming ill in the first place. Some scholars suggest that it was their obedience to dietary and sanitary laws that enabled the Jews to survive the various diseases that wiped out many other ancient peoples.

Likewise the moral law, as embodied in the Ten Commandments, offered similar protection. Those who disregarded it would suffer from spiritual diseases that could in turn result in physical illnesses.

Despite the sophistication of modern medical knowledge, many cures still elude us. If you or someone you love is suffering from a spiritual or physical malady, seek the Lord today for grace and wisdom, remembering always that he is "the LORD who heals you."

Wednesday

PRAYING THE NAME

Surely he took up our infirmities
and carried our sorrows,
yet we considered him stricken by God,
smitten by him, and afflicted.
But he was pierced for our transgressions,
he was crushed for our iniquities;
the punishment that brought us peace was upon him,
and by his wounds we are healed. (Isaiah 53:4–5)

So he cried out to the LORD and the LORD showed him a tree. When he cast it into the waters, the waters were made sweet. (Exodus 15:25 NKJV)

Reflect On: Isaiah 53
Praise God: For his mercy, revealed in the death and resurrection of Jesus.
Offer Thanks: That God did not leave us in our sins.
Confess: Any pride that makes it difficult to admit your sin.
Ask God: To give you a deeper appreciation for the grace of forgiveness.

The Hebrew Scriptures depict God as one who both wounds and heals, who smites his people for their sins to wake them up to their spiritual danger, but who quickly restores them when they repent. If you read Genesis straight through to Malachi, you will find an awful lot of smiting going on but precious little repentance.

Rather than give up on us, God initiated a deeper strategy, one that would not have occurred to us even had we millions of years to ponder the problem. Instead of continuing the endless cycle of smiting and healing, punishing and restoring, God allowed his own Son to be smitten, struck down for our offenses. The tree on which Jesus was impaled is like the tree God instructed Moses to throw into the bitter waters of Marah. This time God plunged his Son into the waters of death. But instead of being swallowed up by them, he rose up alive again, becoming living water for all who seek him.

No wonder there's power in the name of Jesus! Two thousand years after his death, people are still getting healed because of prayer. You can hardly read a major newspaper or magazine without running across another scientific study indicating a positive link between prayer and healing.

If bitter waters are swirling around you or someone you love, if you are battling a physical or emotional illness, remember this: God not only *provides* a remedy but he *is* the remedy. Draw near to *Yahweh Rophe* today, entrusting yourself to the One who has the power to heal you.

Thursday

Praying the Name

As he went along, he saw a man blind from birth. His disciples asked him. "Rabbi, who sinned, this man or his parents, that he was born blind?"

"Neither this man nor his parents sinned," said Jesus, "but this happened so that the work of God might be displayed in his life. As long as it is day, we must do the work of him who sent me. Night is coming, when no one can work. While I am in the world, I am the light of the world." Having said this, he spit on the ground, made some mud with the saliva, and put it on the man's eyes. "Go," he told him, "wash in the Pool of Siloam." . . . So the man went and washed, and came home seeing. (John 9:1–7)

Reflect On:	John 9:1–7
Praise God:	Because his Son Jesus is the light of the world.
Offer Thanks:	For the way God has brought you out of darkness and into the light of his presence.
Confess:	Any tendency to rely merely on your own judgment rather than asking God to help you see clearly through the power of his Spirit.
Ask God:	To uncover areas of spiritual blindness in your life and in the life of the church.

One of Jesus' favorite miracles, it seems, was healing blind people, often in the presence of the spiritually blind. In the case of the man born blind, it wasn't simply a matter of clearing up a problem of blurred vision. The man had never once seen the pale summer sky, the shape of his own footprint, or the features of a single human face. Imagine this same man washing in the Pool of Siloam as Jesus had told him to do, splashing the water on his face and rubbing the mud away, unable to suppress the wild hope that this strange remedy might somehow work. The light would have come on strong at first, like a sudden assault. Then gradually his eyes would have imposed order on a chaotic mix of sensations, separating light from dark, earth from sky—distinguishing shapes, movement, landscapes, people. Perceiving color and texture for the first time, he might have thought the world newly created, just for him.

When this walking miracle of a man returned home, a wonderment to his neighbors, he allowed them to lead him straight to the Pharisees who praised God and threw a party to celebrate his healing! Right? No, incredibly, they challenged him and scolded him and then threw him out of the synagogue! They had liked him better as a blind man and beggar. He had been so little trouble then. Now that he was able to see, he spoke of Jesus as a godly man, a wonder worker, a man whose claims had to be taken seriously. But the Pharisees, the religious experts of their day, would not. Jesus had violated their rules and offended their sensibilities by mixing saliva with mud and then rubbing it on the man's eyes, thus breaking the Sabbath rest. Refusing the evidence of their own eyes, the Pharisees chose to become blind to the compassionate work of God.

When Jesus heard what had happened to the man, he found him and confronted him with this question: "Do you believe in the Son of Man?"

The man replied, saying, "Lord, I believe," and then worshiped him. Having received physical sight, he now had spiritual vision as well.

The healing Jesus offers us today is not merely physical and therefore temporary. His miracles are far more penetrating, like his word, "dividing soul and spirit, joints and marrow; it judges the thoughts and attitudes of the heart" (Hebrews 4:12). Today, as you pray for healing, for yourself or someone you love, listen to the question Jesus is asking: "Do you believe?"

Friday

PROMISES ASSOCIATED WITH GOD'S NAME

Physical healing is a temporary remedy for mortal bodies. Ultimately, God's healing work on this earth points to the healing all of us will receive in heaven, where there will be no such thing as birth defects, cancer, heart disease, arthritis, AIDS, strokes, depression, diabetes, leukemia, hemophilia, asthma, or even the common cold. Yet healing in the here and now is a great blessing, one that can come as the result of faith and prayer. In this world, where "pain" is still a constant part of our vocabulary, we need to hold fast to Yahweh Rophe, asking him to reveal himself as "the LORD who heals us."

Promises in Scripture

This is what the LORD, the God of your father David, says: I have heard your prayer and seen your tears; I will heal you. (2 Kings 20:5)

Praise the LORD, O my soul;
all my inmost being, praise his holy name.
Praise the LORD, O my soul,
and forget not all his benefits—
who forgives all your sins
and heals all your diseases,
who redeems your life from the pit
and crowns you with love and compassion,
who satisfies your desires with good things
so that your youth is renewed like the eagle's. (Psalm 103:1–5)

Jesus said to Jairus, "Don't be afraid; just believe, and she will be healed." (Luke 8:50)

Is any one of you sick? He should call the elders of the church to pray over him and anoint him with oil in the name of the Lord. And the prayer offered in faith will make the sick person well; the Lord will raise him up. (James 5:14–15)

Continued Prayer and Praise

Ask God for forgiveness and healing. (Psalm 38)

Pray for healing. (Isaiah 57:18–20; Jeremiah 17:14)

Remember that Jesus took on himself our infirmities. (Matthew 8:16–17)

Reflect on the ministry of Jesus. (Luke 4:14–19)

Realize God's power to heal the brokenhearted. (Psalm 147:1–6)

9

The Lord My Banner

Yahweh Nissi

The Name

Ancient armies carried standards or banners that served as marks of identification and as symbols that embodied the ideals of a people. A banner, like a flag, was something that could be seen from afar, serving as a rallying point for troops before a battle. Though banners were first used in Egypt, Babylonia, Assyria, and Persia, the Israelites carried them on their march through the desert. When you pray to *Yahweh Nissi,* you are praying to the God who is powerful enough to overcome any foe.

Key Scripture

Moses built an altar and called it The LORD is my Banner. He said, "For hands were lifted up to the throne of the LORD. The LORD will be at war against the Amalekites from generation to generation." (Exodus 17:15–16)

Monday

GOD REVEALS HIS NAME

The Amalekites came and attacked the Israelites at Rephidim. Moses said to Joshua, "Choose some of our men and go out to fight the Amalekites. Tomorrow I will stand on top of the hill with the staff of God in my hands."

So Joshua fought the Amalekites as Moses had ordered, and Moses, Aaron and Hur went to the top of the hill. As long as Moses held up his hands, the Israelites were winning, but whenever he lowered his hands, the Amalekites were winning. When Moses' hands grew tired, they took a stone and put it under him and he sat on it. Aaron and Hur held his hands up—one on one side, one on the other—so that his hands remained steady till sunset. So Joshua overcame the Amalekite army with the sword.

Then the LORD said to Moses, "Write this on a scroll as something to be remembered and make sure that Joshua hears it, because I will completely blot out the memory of Amalek from under heaven."

Moses built an altar and called it The LORD is my Banner. He said, "For hands were lifted up to the throne of the LORD. The LORD will be at war against the Amalekites from generation to generation." (Exodus 17:8–16)

Lord, I thank you for raising your standard over me. Today, as I face spiritual battles of many kinds, help me to be confident of your protection, to fight with your power, to prevail in your strength. Yahweh Nissi, may your victory be total and complete, destroying whatever stands in the way of your plans and purposes. Amen.

Understanding the Name

Unlike fabric flags, ancient banners were usually made out of wood or metal and shaped into various figures or emblems that could be fastened to a bare staff or a long pole. Depicting birds, animals, or gods, they often glistened brightly in the sun so that they could be seen from far off. A banner carried at the head of an army or planted on a high hill served as a rallying point for troops before battle or as an announcement of a victory already won. Because they embodied the ideals and aspirations of whoever carried them, banners aroused devotion to a nation, a cause, or a leader. When Moses held up the staff of God in the battle with the Amalekites, he was holding it like a banner, appealing to God's power. By building an altar and naming it *Yahweh Nissi* (yah-WEH nis-SEE), "The LORD is my Banner," he created a memorial of God's protection and power during the Israelites' first battle after leaving Egypt.

Studying the Name

1. The Amalekites were fierce enemies of the Israelites and the first to attack them after their liberation from Egypt (see Deuteronomy 25:17–19). As members of God's people, we face spiritual enemies intent on destroying God's plans and purposes for our lives. What are some of the enemies you face and how have you dealt with them?
2. What does it mean to engage in spiritual battles today? What difference would it make if you could say, like Moses, "The LORD is my Banner"?

Tuesday

PRAYING THE NAME

Moses built an altar and called it The LORD is my Banner. He said, "For hands were lifted up to the throne of the LORD. The LORD will be at war against the Amalekites from generation to generation." (Exodus 17:15–16)

Reflect On: Exodus 17:8–15
Praise God: Because there is no greater power in heaven or on earth.
Offer Thanks: For God's power at work in your life.
Confess: Your tendency to try to fight your own battles in your own strength.
Ask God: To increase your faith in his desire to use his power on your behalf.

On November 9, 1989, the border between East and West Berlin was suddenly thrown open. Hordes of East Germans rushed to the western part of the city, creating a kind of jubilant chaos. At one border crossing so many people crowded onto an old bridge that it collapsed and another was hastily built to accommodate the crowds. When the Berlin Wall finally came down, the entire world cheered, amazed at how suddenly freedom had come to this communist nation.

Many of us naively thought of this newfound freedom as a kind of "event," as something that had been accomplished the minute the wall was torn down and the old guard run out. We had little idea of the painful process that would ensue as Germany and Russia and other Eastern European countries struggled to adjust to their new freedoms. As one commentator said, demolishing the physical wall was simple. Demolishing the wall in the minds of the people—that would take much longer.

It was the same for the Israelites who had won a certain kind of freedom when they crossed the Red Sea. God dealt a death blow to their Egyptian overlords when Moses raised his staff over the waters, making a divine pathway through the sea. But as the former slaves adjusted to their new freedoms, they discovered numerous internal and external enemies.

Their first battle after leaving Egypt was with the Amalekites. The Amalekite strategy of attacking the weakest and of trying to thwart God's plan for his people made them perpetual enemies of God. When Moses held up the staff of God as Joshua fought against the Amalekites, he was holding a visible sign of God's power, like a banner, for all the people to see. Whenever his hands grew tired and he lowered the staff, the Amalekites began winning. That's when Aaron and Hur began supporting his hands so the Israelites would not waver in their battle.

But what relevance does this ancient story have today? If you picture the Amalekites as a symbol of all the forces that oppose God, you begin to realize the spiritual battles that still face us. Just as the Israelites were freed from their bondage to Egypt, we are freed from bondage to sin and Satan the moment we surrender ourselves to Christ. But we still face countless battles on our way to the promised land of heaven. Some of the worst of these are internal, as we struggle to overcome the dividing wall in our own souls—a kind of spiritual ambivalence that makes us easy prey for our enemies. Today as you face spiritual battles of many kinds, remember to hold high the banner of God's power, knowing that he alone gives the victory no matter how fierce the enemy.

Wednesday

Praying the Name

The Lord said to Moses, "Make a snake and put it up on a pole; anyone who is bitten can look at it and live." So Moses made a bronze snake and put it up on a pole. Then when anyone was bitten by a snake and looked at the bronze snake, he lived. (Numbers 21:8–9)

Just as Moses lifted up the snake in the desert, so the Son of Man must be lifted up, that everyone who believes in him may have eternal life. (John 3:14–15)

His banner over me is love. (Song of Songs 2:4)

Reflect On:	Numbers 21:4–9
Praise God:	For the gift of his Son.
Offer Thanks:	That God provided a remedy for our sin.
Confess:	Any complaints or bitterness you may have harbored toward God.
Ask God:	To increase your faith in his goodness and his love.

Freedom is a sweet word in any language, especially to a nation of slaves. Still its power to motivate waned during the Israelite's long journey toward the Promised Land. By now they had spent nearly forty years trudging around in the desert. Setting up camp and settling in for a time. Then breaking camp and marching on endlessly, tribe by tribe and clan by clan. After years of wandering and wondering when they would reach a homeland, they lost faith completely and complained bitterly. As always, their complaints were exaggerated.

- God hated them.
- Moses was a fool.
- The manna from heaven tasted like garbage.
- Life had been so much better in Egypt.

Imagining ourselves in the place of the Israelites, it's hard not to sympathize. But God didn't. Instead he punished them, sending a plague of deadly snakes. Terrified, the people repented, begging forgiveness for calling God cruel and uncaring, for rejecting his servant, Moses, for spurning his grace and rejecting his plan. They had called good evil and evil good. Then the Lord told Moses to make a bronze snake and put it up on a pole. Anyone who had been bitten by a snake had only to look at the metal snake to be healed.

A strange story. A strange remedy. Stranger still, the Hebrew word for "pole" (*nes*) can also be translated as "banner." So the bronze snake was a banner that Moses lifted up over the people, calling them together to be healed of their faithlessness. Calling them together so that God and they could have the victory over their sin.

Later, John's gospel applies this powerful image to Jesus—to the act of his crucifixion. Today, as you ponder the meaning of *Yahweh Nissi*, remember the cross. Remember that it is by his wounds that we are healed and the bite of sin is rendered harmless. Receive his forgiveness. For his banner over you is love.

Thursday

PRAYING THE NAME

"See, I will beckon to the Gentiles,
I will lift up my banner to the peoples;
they will bring your sons in their arms
and carry your daughters on their shoulders. . . .
Then you will know that I am the LORD;
those who hope in me will not be disappointed."
Can plunder be taken from warriors,
or captives rescued from the fierce?
But this is what the LORD *says:*
"Yes, captives will be taken from warriors,
and plunder retrieved from the fierce;
I will contend with those who contend with you,
and your children I will save." (Isaiah 49:22–25)

Reflect On: Isaiah 49:22–25
Praise God: For his power to save the children in your life.
Offer Thanks: For God's promise of help.
Confess: Any lack of faith, fueled by disappointment.
Ask God: To arouse your fighting spirit on behalf of your children.

Though you may be living for Christ, your children or children you care about may not be. You may have done your best to share your faith when they were young—reading the Bible, teaching them to pray, bringing them to church, and modeling the love of Christ. Yet they strayed, pulled away by a thousand enticements.

Year after year you pray, but little seems to happen. Things may have even gotten worse. Sex, money, drugs, partying, illness, apathy—whatever it is, you know your loved ones will self-destruct if they do not find their way back to God. Perhaps you have become so discouraged by what you see that you have stopped praying.

Yet Scripture tells us that those who hope in God will not be disappointed. Notice that it doesn't say those who hope in God *usually* won't be disappointed. It flat out says they *will not* be disappointed. That means that *ultimately* you won't be disappointed in God's faithfulness even if your children, grandchildren, nieces, nephews, or neighbors are failing in school or living on the streets or engaged in illicit relationships or drinking themselves to death or working so hard that they have no time for God. You may agonize over their choices and their circumstances, but you can't afford to let that agony push you into premature conclusions about where they will end up. The whole story has yet to be written, and it can still be influenced by your hope and by your prayers. Disappointment is nothing but a premature conclusion, causing you to stop reading before the story's end, making you abandon your hope in God, and enfeebling your ability to pray.

Instead of giving up, pray that *Yahweh Nissi* will unfurl his banner for all to see, rescuing these children from whatever captivates them. Join with other prayerful people—parents, teachers, aunts and uncles, grandparents, and neighbors—to remind God of his promise to contend with those who contend with you—to save the children you love and to bring them home again.

Friday

PROMISES ASSOCIATED WITH GOD'S NAME

In the spring of 2002, in the midst of a Holy Week wracked by violence, came this reminder from the leaders of the historic churches in the Holy Land: "Our own land has experienced a great deal of bloodshed and violence, especially in these past months. But to what avail? . . . the way of Jesus is quite different. The triumph he achieved that first Holy Week and Easter did not arise from human strength but rather from the strength that comes from God. . . . The Cross should remind us that it is in this sign we conquer."

Indeed, "the way of Jesus is quite different." His cross must become more than a pretty piece of jewelry or an adornment for the walls of our homes. It must become a banner around which we rally and by which we live. In his cross we have the power to conquer.

Promises in Scripture

In that day the Root of Jesse will stand as a banner for the peoples; the nations will rally to him, and his place of rest will be glorious. In that day the Lord will reach out his hand a second time to reclaim the remnant that is left of his people. . . . He will raise a banner for the nations and gather the exiles of Israel. (Isaiah 11:10–12)

But for those who fear you, you have raised a banner
to be unfurled against the bow. (Psalm 60:4)

For the trumpet will sound, the dead will be raised imperishable, and we will be changed. . . . Then the saying that is written will come true: "Death has been swallowed up in victory."

"Where, O death, is your victory?
Where, O death, is your sting?"

The sting of death is sin, and the power of sin is the law. But thanks be to God! He gives us the victory through our Lord Jesus Christ. (1 Corinthians 15:52, 54–57)

Continued Prayer and Praise

Ask for God's help in the midst of difficulty. (Psalm 20)

Let the cross of Christ be the banner under which you live. (1 Corinthians 1:18)

10

Consuming Fire, Jealous God

אֵשׁ אֹכְלָה אֵל קַנָּא

Esh Oklah, El Kanna

The Names

The Lord is a Consuming Fire who will ultimately destroy whatever is opposed to his holiness. He is also a Jealous God, who loves us completely and who, therefore, demands our wholehearted response. If we love him, we can be confident of his mercy, and our own zeal will make us jealous for God's honor and glory. When you pray these names of God, ask him to give you and the church a deeper understanding of his holiness and a greater desire to honor and exalt his name.

Key Scriptures

Do not worship any other god, for the LORD, whose name is Jealous, is a jealous God. (Exodus 34:14)

Be careful not to forget the covenant of the LORD your God that he made with you; do not make for yourselves an idol in the form of anything the LORD your God has forbidden. For the LORD your God is a consuming fire, a jealous God. (Deuteronomy 4:23–24)

Monday

GOD REVEALS HIS NAME

Then the LORD said: "I am making a covenant with you. Before all your people I will do wonders never before done in any nation in all the world. The people you live among will see how awesome is the work that I, the LORD, will do for you. Obey what I command you today. I will drive out before you the Amorites, Canaanites, Hittites, Perizzites, Hivites and Jebusites. Be careful not to make a treaty with those who live in the land where you are going, or they will be a snare among you. Break down their altars, smash their sacred stones and cut down their Asherah poles. Do not worship any other god, for the LORD, whose name is Jealous, is a jealous God. (Exodus 34:10–14)

Be careful not to forget the covenant of the LORD your God that he made with you; do not make for yourselves an idol in the form of anything the LORD your God has forbidden. For the LORD your God is a consuming fire, a jealous God. (Deuteronomy 4:23–24)

Fear the LORD your God, serve him only and take your oaths in his name. Do not follow other gods, the gods of the peoples around you; for the LORD your God, who is among you, is a jealous God and his anger will burn against you, and he will destroy you from the face of the land. Do not test the LORD your God as you did at Massah. Be sure to keep the commands of the LORD your God and the stipulations and decrees he has given you. Do what is right and good in the LORD's sight, so that it may go well with you and you may go in and take over the good land that the LORD promised on oath to your forefathers, thrusting out all your enemies before you, as the LORD said. (Deuteronomy 6:13–19)

Lord, you are holy beyond my understanding, perfect in a way I cannot perceive. Help me to catch a glimpse of your glory and to grow more zealous for your name, that I might exalt it by the way I live and the way I love. Send your refining fire to heal and purge my heart and send your all-consuming love to lead me home. Amen.

Understanding the Name

God sometimes manifested himself through images of fire—as a blazing torch, in the burning bush, or as a pillar of fire. When Moses met with God on Mount Sinai, the Israelites thought the glory of the Lord looked like a consuming fire on top of the mountain.

Most often, when Scripture pictures God as a consuming fire [*Esh Oklah*; AISH o-KLAH], it is in connection with expressions of divine anger against the sins of men and nations. Even so, his jealousy is not the "green-eyed monster" so often associated with human jealousy. As biblical scholar Edward Mac pointed out: "This word ... did not bear the evil meaning now associated with it in our usage, but rather signified 'righteous zeal,' Jehovah's zeal for His own name or glory."

Even so, Scripture compares God's jealousy to what a husband feels when his wife has been unfaithful. No wonder the first of the Ten Commandments prohibits the worship of other gods. The Lord is our Jealous God [*El Kanna*; EL kan-NAH], who cannot endure unfaithfulness. Jesus expressed this same kind of exclusiveness when he told his disciples: "I am the way and the truth and the life. No one comes to the Father except through me. If you really knew me, you would know my Father as well. From now on, you do know him and have seen him" (John 14:6–7).

Studying the Name

1. What promises does God make in the Exodus passage? What commands does he give? What warnings does he issue?

2. Why do you think the Lord says his name is "Jealous"?
3. What is the significance of this particular title of God in relation to his covenant?
4. How does this name of God relate to your own life? To the church today?

Tuesday

Praying the Name

Then King Nebuchadnezzar leaped to his feet in amazement and asked his advisers, "Weren't there three men that we tied up and threw into the fire?"

They replied, "Certainly, O king."

He said, "Look! I see four men walking around in the fire, unbound and unharmed, and the fourth looks like a son of the gods." (Daniel 3: 24–25)

"I myself will be a wall of fire around it [Jerusalem]," declares the Lord, *"and I will be its glory within." (Zechariah 2:5)*

Reflect On:	Daniel 3:1–25; Zechariah 2:5
Praise God:	For his purity.
Offer Thanks:	For God's protecting power.
Confess:	Any tendency to compromise your faith in order to fit into the world around you.
Ask God:	To bless and protect those who are being persecuted because of their faith in him.

Once upon a time in Babylon King Nebuchadnezzar constructed an enormous golden idol to honor the Babylonian god Nabu. Then the great king issued an order: Everyone in Babylon from the least to the greatest must fall flat on his face to worship the great golden god. Anyone who defied his order would be burned up in an enormous furnace.

Remarkably, three young Jewish men refused. Enraged by the calm defiance of Shadrach, Meshach, and Abednego, Nebuchadnezzar ordered the furnace heated to seven times its normal intensity.

Binding the young men, his soldiers threw them into the furnace, no doubt surprised to find that they would become its first victims.

When Nebuchadnezzar peered into the furnace, he saw an astonishing sight: "four men walking around in the fire, unbound and unharmed." And the fourth, he remarked, "looks like a son of the gods."

Notice in this dramatic and ironic story how God's judgment is revealed. First of all, Nebuchadnezzar's anger backfires. By turning up the heat to reflect his rage, he unwittingly destroys his own soldiers. By contrast the flames are rendered powerless against the three young men whose zeal for God led them to refuse his command.

To oppose God is to encounter him ultimately as a terror, a God who in his wrath against sin is like a consuming fire. By contrast, to love God is to encounter him as a caring God, who stands, as Zechariah says, like a "wall of fire" to protect and deliver us. No wonder the three young men told Nebuchadnezzar they had no need to defend themselves.

As you search your heart in God's presence today, ask for the grace to remain faithful, regardless of external pressures to compromise or abandon your faith. Realize, too, that many thousands of Christians throughout the world still suffer extreme persecution because of their faith. Ask God to be a "wall of fire" around them, to protect and deliver them. To make your praying more effective, you may want to use this watch list of the ten countries in the world where Christians are most persecuted, noting either their form of government or their primary religious affiliation.

1. North Korea—communism
2. Saudi Arabia—Islam
3. Laos—communism
4. Vietnam—communism
5. Iran—Islam
6. Turkmenistan—Islam
7. Maldives—Islam

8. Bhutan—Buddhism
9. Myanmar—Buddhism
10. China—communism

Consider adopting one of these countries to pray for on a regular basis. Conducting a little research about the political, cultural, and religious background of your chosen country will enable you to pray more effectively and motivate you to keep praying.

Wednesday

Praying the Name

But who can endure the day of his coming? Who can stand when he appears? For he will be like a refiner's fire or a launderer's soap. He will sit as a refiner and purifier of silver; he will purify the Levites and refine them like gold and silver. (Malachi 3:2–3)

Therefore, since we are receiving a kingdom that cannot be shaken, let us be thankful, and so worship God acceptably with reverence and awe, for our "God is a consuming fire." (Hebrews 12:28–29)

Reflect On: Malachi 3:2–3 and Hebrews 12:28–29
Praise God: For his righteous anger.
Offer Thanks: For the mercy God has shown you.
Confess: Any complacency about sin.
Ask God: To purify you.

Anyone who has ever worked in publishing as I have will realize that you cannot force-feed books to prospective readers. That's why the publisher of a series of small devotional books with titles like *A Touch of His Joy, A Touch of His Wisdom,* and *A Touch of His Presence* didn't say yes to my wry suggestion for a volume entitled *A Touch of His Wrath.* Who on earth would want to read such a book?

But despite our distaste for the subject, Scripture tells us in both Old and New Testaments that there is such a thing as God's wrath. Believing in God's mercy and grace does not mean believing there is no longer any such thing as divine anger. God sent his Son to save us, but we can only be saved if we choose to be. As Ignatius of Antioch put it in the first century, "We must either fear his future wrath or love his present grace—one of the two!" Anyone who persistently ignores God, resists him, flaunts his law, or rejects the salvation he offers will ultimately incur his wrath.

But what does it mean to talk about God's anger? Is God prone to throwing celestial tantrums to get his way? Hardly, for God's anger is not rooted in selfish concern, nor is it randomly or recklessly expressed. Rather God's anger, which Scripture sometimes describes as a "consuming fire," is an expression of his justice and his holiness. Its primary purpose is restorative, to bring his creatures back to himself, or, failing that, to restore the proper relationship between sin and its consequences in order to preserve his justice and holiness.

Knowing that Jesus has saved us from God's wrath is always a cause for great rejoicing but never a cause for smugness. We need to remember that the people who angered Jesus the most were always religious people—people who knew God's laws but twisted them to serve their purposes and then judged others for falling short. Today as you think about God as a Consuming Fire, join me in praying for the grace to recognize and repent of sin. Let us ask God to consume everything in our lives that distracts from his glory. Then we can pray for those in our world who seem far from God, that they will heed the warning of his wrath and receive the salvation he offers through his Son.

Thursday

Praying the Name

Do not worship any other god, for the Lord, whose name is Jealous, is a jealous God. (Exodus 34:14)

Place me like a seal over your heart,
like a seal on your arm;
for love is as strong as death,
its jealousy unyielding as the grave.
It burns like blazing fire,
like a mighty flame.
Many waters cannot quench love;
rivers cannot wash it away.
If one were to give
all the wealth of his house for love,
it would be utterly scorned. (Song of Songs 8:6–7)

Reflect On: Exodus 34:14; Song of Songs 8:6–7
Praise God: Who is worthy of praise.
Offer Thanks: For the ways God has pursued you.
Confess: Any tendency to run away from God.
Ask God: To increase your love for him.

Shakespeare described jealousy as a "green-eyed monster." Mark Twain called it the "trademark of small minds." Robert Heinlein labeled it a "symptom of neurotic insecurity." Such apt but unattractive descriptions of human jealousy will only confuse you if you try to apply them to God, whose jealousy might better be described by the words of the English poet Joseph Addison: "Jealousy is that pain which a man feels from the apprehension that he is not equally beloved by the person whom he entirely loves."

This is the kind of jealousy that impels God to pursue us, despite our evasions, our indifference, or our waywardness. Francis Thompson was a nineteenth-century poet, an opium addict, whose sense of the divine pursuit of his soul is famously captured in his poem *The Hound of Heaven*:

> *Adown Titanic glooms of chasméd fears,*
> *From those strong Feet that followed, followed after.*
> *But with unhurrying chase,*
> *And unperturbéd pace,*
> *Deliberate speed, majestic instancy,*
> *They beat—and a Voice beat*
> *More instant than the Feet—*
> *"All things betray thee, who betrayest Me."*

Francis's struggle with the great hound who pursued his fleeing soul provides a vivid picture of the way in which God pursues us—relentlessly, shrewdly, passionately. He is a Lover who will not be satisfied until we return his love with equal passion.

Take time today to think about the ways God has pursued you throughout your lifetime. Ask him to help you recognize how he has been at work. Then pray for the grace to forsake every love that would compete with your love for him.

Pray, too, for friends and family members whom God is pursuing. Urge him to be relentless in revealing his love and capturing their hearts. Then be relentless in your prayers on their behalf.

Friday

PROMISES ASSOCIATED WITH GOD'S NAME

Tolerance is a popular word these days. And no wonder. We live in a pluralistic society made up of people from a rich variety of cultural, ethnic, and religious backgrounds. We need to respect each other in order to live peaceably. But when "tolerance" becomes an excuse for erasing important distinctions, we wander into slippery territory both intellectually and spiritually.

This is especially true when it comes to matters of faith. You can't sprinkle a little Hinduism on top of New Age notions, mix together ideas from Buddhist cosmology with Christian theology, toss in a few Jewish proverbs, stir it all up, and call it religion. It may be fashionable, but it's not faith. Faith is more rigorous. It doesn't respond to market forces or to the latest trends. Real faith arises from contact with the living God, who by his own definition is jealous for our attention, our devotion, our love. He's not interested in competing with other deities. He neither shares his glory nor compromises his holiness. This is our Jealous God, the one who loves us with an everlasting, all-consuming love.

Promises in Scripture

Be careful not to forget the covenant of the LORD your God that he made with you; do not make for yourselves an idol in the form of anything the LORD your God has forbidden. For the LORD your God is a consuming fire, a jealous God. (Deuteronomy 4:23–24)

Who of us can dwell with the consuming fire?
Who of us can dwell with everlasting burning?
He who walks righteously
and speaks what is right. (Isaiah 33:14–15)

Continued Prayer and Praise

Consuming Fire

Realize that God's glory is like a consuming fire. (Exodus 24:15)

Pray for God's help. (Psalm 18:6–17)

Jealous God

Remember that the Lord our God is a jealous God. (Deuteronomy 5:8–10)

Call on the name of the Lord and strive to take hold of him. (Isaiah 64:1–8)

11

Holy One of Israel

Qedosh Yisrael

The Name

The title "Holy One of Israel" emphasizes God's uniqueness, otherness, and mystery as well as his call to his people to become holy as he is. The Israelites were to be set apart for God, devoted to his service, and committed to honoring his character by reflecting it in all their relationships. In the New Testament Jesus was recognized as the Holy One of God by demons who were threatened by his power and purity. As believers, we are called to reflect the character of Christ, to be holy even as he is holy.

When you pray to the Holy One of Israel, you are praying to the God whose holiness not only encompasses his separation from evil, but his power, knowledge, justice, mercy, goodness, and love.

Key Scripture

The Lord said to Moses, "Speak to the entire assembly of Israel and say to them: 'Be holy because I, the Lord your God, am holy.'" (Leviticus 19:1–2)

Monday

God Reveals His Name

The Lord said to Moses, "Speak to the entire assembly of Israel and say to them: 'Be holy because I, the Lord your God, am holy.

"'Each of you must respect his mother and father, and you must observe my Sabbaths. I am the Lord your God.

"'Do not turn to idols or make gods of cast metal for yourselves. I am the Lord your God. . . .

"'When you reap the harvest of your land, do not reap to the very edges of your field or gather the gleanings of your harvest. Do not go over your vineyard a second time or pick up the grapes that have fallen. Leave them for the poor and the alien. I am the Lord your God.

"'Do not steal.

"'Do not lie.

"'Do not deceive one another.

"'Do not swear falsely by my name and so profane the name of your God. I am the Lord.

"'Do not defraud your neighbor or rob him.

"'Do not hold back the wages of a hired man overnight.

"'Do not curse the deaf or put a stumbling block in front of the blind, but fear your God. I am the Lord.

"'Do not pervert justice; do not show partiality to the poor or favoritism to the great, but judge your neighbor fairly.

"'Do not go about spreading slander among your people.

"'Do not do anything that endangers your neighbor's life. I am the Lord.

"'Do not hate your brother in your heart. Rebuke your neighbor frankly so you will not share in his guilt.

"'Do not seek revenge or bear a grudge against one of your people, but love your neighbor as yourself. I am the Lord.'" (Leviticus 19:1–4, 9–18)

Lord, your commandments reveal your character. Help us to reflect you in everything we do. Cleanse us and remake us into the image of your Son by the power of your Spirit. Help us to strive after holiness, knowing that to be holy is to glorify your name. Amen.

Understanding the Name

Qedosh is Hebrew for "Holy One," a title for God that appears most frequently in the book of Isaiah, though it also appears in some of the other prophets, notably Hosea, Jeremiah, Ezekiel, and Habakkuk, and in Psalms and Job. It emphasizes God's otherness, separateness, and mystery. The term most frequently used for "holy" in the New Testament is *hagios.*

To understand the title "Holy One of Israel," *Qedosh Yisrael* (ke-DOSH yis-ra-AIL), we need first to understand that holiness is grounded in God's nature. It refers not to one of his attributes but to the totality of his perfection. In his holiness, God exists above and apart from the world he has made.

Things, times, places, people, and other created beings became holy by virtue of their connection to God. Thus, the people of Israel became holy because God chose them. Their holiness was to be expressed and maintained through ritual practices and adherence to moral laws, which set them apart for the service of God.

It is important to realize that God's holiness involves not just separation from sin but his absolute hostility toward it. Christ ultimately bridged the chasm between God and sinful human beings by making himself the perfect offering for our sins. Believers are called to be holy as he is holy and are enabled to imitate Christ by the grace of the Holy Spirit.

Studying the Word

1. In Leviticus 19, God links his commandments to his name. Why do you think he keeps reminding the people that he is "the LORD your God"?

2. If this were the only passage of Scripture you had ever read, what would it lead you to believe about God's character?
3. Read through these commandments prayerfully, asking the Holy Spirit to show you where you need to make changes in order to live according to God's guidelines for holiness. What areas in your life are highlighted?

Tuesday

PRAYING THE NAME

In the year that King Uzziah died, I saw the Lord seated on a throne, high and exalted, and the train of his robe filled the temple. Above him were seraphs, each with six wings: With two wings they covered their faces, with two they covered their feet, and with two they were flying. And they were calling to one another:

> *"Holy, holy, holy is the* LORD *Almighty;*
> *the whole earth is full of his glory."*

At the sound of their voices the doorposts and thresholds shook and the temple was filled with smoke.

"Woe to me!" I cried. "I am ruined! For I am a man of unclean lips, and live among a people of unclean lips, and my eyes have seen the King, the LORD *Almighty."*

Then one of the seraphs flew to me with a live coal in his hand, which he had taken with tongs from the altar. . . . "See, this has touched your lips; your guilt is taken away and your sin atoned for." (Isaiah 6:1–7)

Reflect On: Isaiah 6:1–7
Praise God: For his perfect holiness.
Offer Thanks: That there is a perfect correspondence between God's nature and his actions.
Confess: Your lack of reverence.
Ask God: To reveal his holiness to you more clearly.

Mathematical models indicate that the sun, a rather small star, is about twenty-seven million degrees Fahrenheit at its core. And even though the sun is ninety-three million miles away, we earthlings still suffer burns unless we take proper precautions, even on cloudy days.

Given the sun's fantastic heat, it isn't hard to imagine what would happen were it to move suddenly closer to earth, pitching in our direction.

Nearly three thousand years ago a man named Isaiah had a vision of God so vivid that he must have felt as though the sun itself had suddenly come hurtling through the atmosphere. So overpowering was his sense of God's presence that Isaiah felt certain he was ruined, about to be destroyed.

But why should looking at God destroy a man? In the presence of holiness, Isaiah immediately saw his sin—and his danger—for he would have perceived not only God's complete lack of sin but his utter opposition toward it. And, as Addison Leitch has said, "There is a sense in which God cannot help himself when he resists anything in the universe that is contrary to his own nature."

Fortunately, God provided a way for Isaiah to be cleansed of his guilt so that he could live and proclaim the word of the Lord regardless of whether people were ready to hear it.

If nothing else, the remarkable account of Isaiah's vision should cause us to wonder whether we take God altogether too lightly, whether we have the faintest notion of his greatness or the slightest perception of how stunning is the privilege of belonging to him. Perhaps it is time to cover our eyes, fall on our knees, and proclaim with the heavenly beings, "Holy, holy, holy is the LORD Almighty; the whole earth is full of his glory!"

Wednesday

PRAYING THE NAME

The LORD said to Moses, "Speak to the entire assembly of Israel and say to them: 'Be holy because I, the LORD your God, am holy.'" (Leviticus 19:1)

As obedient children, do not conform to the evil desires you had when you lived in ignorance. But just as he who called you is holy, so be holy in all you do; for it is written: "Be holy, because I am holy." (1 Peter 1:14–16)

Reflect On: Leviticus 19:1–4, 9–18
Praise God: For being generous, honest, truthful, just, and loving.
Offer Thanks: That God has given us in Christ the power to become holy.
Confess: Any tolerance of habitual sin in your life.
Ask God: To help you see the value of living a holy life.

In the first book of C. S. Lewis's classic Chronicles of Narnia, the Lion Aslan gathers around him a solemn circle of animals in the new world of Narnia. Two children watch the proceedings from a distance:

> The Lion opened his mouth, but no sound came from it; he was breathing out, a long warm breath; it seemed to sway all the beasts as the wind sways a line of trees. Far overhead from beyond the veil of blue sky which hid them the stars sang again; a pure, cold, difficult music. Then there came a swift flash like fire (but it burnt nobody) either from the sky or from the Lion itself, and every drop of blood tingled

> in the children's bodies, and the deepest, wildest voice they had ever heard was saying:
>
> "Narnia, Narnia, Narnia, awake. Love. Think. Speak." . . .
>
> Out of the trees wild people stepped forth. . . . And all these and all the beasts and birds in their different voices, low or high or thick or clear, replied:
>
> "Hail, Aslan. We hear and obey. We are awake. We love. We think. We speak. We know." . . .
>
> "Creatures, I give you yourselves," said the strong, happy voice of Aslan. "I give to you forever this land of Narnia. I give you the woods, the fruits, the rivers. I give you the stars and I give you myself. The Dumb Beasts whom I have not chosen are yours also. Treat them gently and cherish them but do not go back to their ways lest you cease to be Talking Beasts. For out of them you were taken and into them you can return. Do not so."

This picture of the newly awakened animals of Narnia is evocative of other awakenings, particularly the spiritual awakening that occurs when we come into a personal relationship with Christ. Suddenly the world has changed. We begin to love, think, know, and speak in ways we never did before. Our former notions about life disintegrate in the face of our experience of God. His attractions are so powerful that we are willing to forsake everything in order to live for him. We want to be holy because we know that to be holy is to be like him and to be near him.

But sometimes we drift. Pleasure entices us. Troubles mount. Sin calls. The world beckons. We wonder why our hearts seem empty and cold. What happened to the zeal we had? What happened to our desire to live an extraordinary life? Why are we sliding back into old habits and patterns? These may be questions the Holy Spirit is urging us to consider. Perhaps he is right now shaking us awake from our spiritual torpor, reminding us that without holiness no one will see the Lord (see Hebrews 12:14). Today let us ask God to help us live out our faith with passionate commitment, fueled by a hunger for holiness that reflects our love of God and his greater love for us. Let us pray earnestly and eagerly for the grace to be fully awake to God's life within us.

Thursday

PRAYING THE NAME

I have written you in my letter not to associate with sexually immoral people—not at all meaning the people of this world who are immoral, or the greedy and swindlers, or idolaters. In that case you would have to leave this world. But now I am writing you that you must not associate with anyone who calls himself a brother but is sexually immoral or greedy, an idolater or a slanderer, a drunkard or a swindler. With such a man do not even eat.

What business is it of mine to judge those outside the church? Are you not to judge those inside? God will judge those outside. "Expel the wicked man from among you." (1 Corinthians 5:9–13)

Reflect On: 1 Corinthians 5:9–13
Praise God: Because his judgments are perfect.
Offer Thanks: That God has put you in touch with people who don't yet know him.
Confess: Any tendency to judge people outside the church.
Ask God: To help you trust his power to transform lives.

It's difficult to live in Michigan if you are a boat lover without a boat. A few years ago, I was able to rectify that problem by purchasing a boat that we keep at a nearby marina. That's when I learned that marinas are tight communities. When you're anchored a few feet away from a boat that's anchored a few feet away from another boat and so on, you get to know people.

Aside from nearly crashing into a few docks that first summer, we had a great time. But by the next summer, I was a little wary, unsure of how to relate to two gay women who had moved to our dock with their brand-new boat, particularly since I didn't want to have to explain their relationship to my preschoolers. I tried avoiding them but that didn't work because they were the friendliest and most helpful people on a dock of friendly people.

Before long, I realized that my attitude toward these two was off-kilter. I had been guilty of doing exactly what Paul warned the Corinthian church not to do—of attempting to separate myself from those outside the church whose behavior didn't match my standards. But Paul says to do that, you'd need to die—to exit the planet! And why on earth would I expect someone to act like Christ when they don't have a relationship with him?

As it sooner or later does, the obvious dawned on me—that holiness involves separating myself, not from a world of sinful people, but from the sinful attitudes and patterns so prevalent in my own life. My task was not to convince this couple of their mistake but simply to love them and to share my faith whenever the opportunity arose. I knew, too, that loving them didn't mean adopting an "anything goes" attitude. I could befriend them without caving in to a relativistic worldview.

It's so easy to equate holiness with a set of outward behaviors, to slip into a self-righteous, "holier than thou" attitude that alienates people from the gospel. But Jesus, the holiest person who ever lived, came not to condemn us—as though giving sin the last word in our lives—but to liberate us from the grip of sin.

As Mother Teresa of Calcutta once said: "Holiness does not consist in doing extraordinary things. It consists in accepting, with a smile, what Jesus sends us. It consists in accepting and following the will of God." Perhaps in addition to accepting *what* Jesus sends us, we need also to accept *who* Jesus sends us.

Friday

PROMISES ASSOCIATED WITH GOD'S NAME

If you had to choose between two substances—stone or flesh—which would you describe as "impervious" or "impenetrable"? The simple answer, of course, would be stone. But it seems that God found stone a far more malleable substance when it came to inscribing his law. To write his law on steely human hearts would take more than the display of divine power Moses witnessed on Mount Sinai. It would take the display of divine love witnessed on Mount Calvary—the death of Jesus.

Two thousand years later, God is still keeping his promise to put his law in our minds and to write it on our hearts. Because of Christ's perfect sacrifice, we not only know God's law but have the power to live by it.

Promises in Scripture

"This is the covenant I will make with the house of Israel
after that time," declares the LORD.
"I will put my law in their minds
and write it on their hearts.
I will be their God,
and they will be my people." (Jeremiah 31:33)

. . . by one sacrifice he [Christ] has made perfect forever those who are being made holy.

The Holy Spirit also testifies to us about this. First he says:

"This is the covenant I will make with them
after that time, says the Lord.
I will put my laws in their hearts,
And I will write them on their minds." (Hebrews 10:14–16)

For God so loved the world that he gave his one and only Son, that whoever believes in him shall not perish but have eternal life. For God did not send his Son into the world to condemn the world, but to save the world through him. (John 3:16–17)

Continued Prayer and Praise

Know that God is the Holy One. (Hosea 11:1–9)

Remember that without holiness, no one will see God. (Hebrews 12:14–24)

Praise Jesus because he is the Holy One. (Luke 1:35–36)

12

The Lord Is Peace

Yahweh Shalom

The Name

Shalom is a Hebrew word, so much richer in its range of meanings than the English word "peace," which usually refers to the absence of outward conflict or to a state of inner calm. The concept of *shalom* includes these ideas but goes beyond them, meaning "wholeness," "completeness," "finished word," "perfection," "safety," or "wellness." *Shalom* comes from living in harmony with God. The fruit of that harmony is harmony with others, prosperity, health, satisfaction, soundness, wholeness, and well-being. When you pray to *Yahweh Shalom,* you are praying to the source of all peace. No wonder his Son is called the Prince of Peace.

Key Scripture

So Gideon built an altar to the LORD there and called it The LORD is Peace. (Judges 6:24)

Monday

GOD REVEALS HIS NAME

Again the Israelites did evil in the eyes of the LORD, and for seven years he gave them into the hands of the Midianites. Because the power of Midian was so oppressive, the Israelites prepared shelters for themselves in mountain clefts, caves and strongholds. . . .

The angel of the LORD came and sat down under the oak in Ophrah that belonged to Joash . . . where his son Gideon was threshing wheat in a winepress to keep it from the Midianites. When the angel of the LORD appeared to Gideon, he said, "The LORD is with you, mighty warrior."

"But sir," Gideon replied, "if the LORD is with us, why has all this happened to us? Where are all his wonders that our fathers told us about when they said, 'Did not the LORD bring us up out of Egypt?' But now the LORD has abandoned us and put us into the hand of Midian."

The LORD turned to him and said, "Go in the strength you have and save Israel out of Midian's hand. Am I not sending you?"

"But Lord," Gideon asked, "how can I save Israel? My clan is the weakest in Manasseh, and I am the least in my family."

The LORD answered, "I will be with you, and you will strike down all the Midianites together."

Gideon replied, "If now I have found favor in your eyes, give me a sign that it is really you talking to me. . . ."

Gideon went in, prepared a young goat, and from an ephah of flour he made bread without yeast. Putting the meat in a basket and its broth in a pot, he brought them out and offered them to him under the oak.

The angel of God said to him, "Take the meat and the unleavened bread, place them on this rock, and pour out the broth." And Gideon did so. With the tip of the staff that was in his hand, the angel of the LORD touched the meat and the unleavened bread. Fire flared from the rock, consuming the meat and the bread. And the angel of the LORD disappeared. When Gideon realized that it was the angel of the LORD, he exclaimed, "Ah, Sovereign LORD! I have seen the angel of the LORD face to face!"

But the LORD said to him, "Peace! Do not be afraid. You are not going to die."

So Gideon built an altar to the LORD there and called it The LORD is Peace. (From Judges 6)

Lord, I long for peace, the peace that only you can give. Please help me to pray for peace throughout the world and peace within my own heart. Help me to do the things I need to in order to experience true shalom. Amen.

Understanding the Name

Yahweh Shalom (yah-WEH sha-LOME) is a title rather than a name of God. *Shalom* is a common term for greeting or farewell in modern Israel. When you say *shalom*, you are not simply saying "Hello," or "Have a Good Day." In its deepest meaning, it expresses the hope that the person may be well in every sense of the word—fulfilled, satisfied, prosperous, healthy, and in harmony with themselves, others, and God. *Shalom* is a covenant word, an expression of God's faithful relationship with his people.

Studying the Name

1. What does this passage reveal about the way God deals with his people's unfaithfulness?
2. Think about a time in your life when you felt harassed by circumstances. What caused your difficulties and how did you respond to them?
3. Why do you think the angel called Gideon a "mighty warrior"?
4. What comes to mind when you hear the word *peace*?

Tuesday

PRAYING THE NAME

When Gideon realized that it was the angel of the LORD, he exclaimed, "Ah, Sovereign LORD! I have seen the angel of the LORD face to face!"

But the LORD said to him, "Peace! Do not be afraid. You are not going to die."

So Gideon built an altar to the LORD there and called it The LORD is Peace. (Judges 6:22–24)

Reflect On:	Judges 6:1–24
Praise God:	For his power to deliver us.
Offer Thanks:	For punishments that bring us back to God.
Confess:	Any patterns in your life that keep you from experiencing God's peace.
Ask God:	To free you from spiritual oppression.

God's people were in a miserable bind. They were living in the Promised Land without enjoying the promised blessings—the milk and honey, the wheat and barley, the peace and prosperity. For seven years Midianite raiders swarmed over their land like locusts, stealing everything in sight. Freed from slavery in Egypt, their idolatry had made them vulnerable to a new oppressor. Finally the Israelites cried out for relief, and God supplied a deliverer in the shape of Gideon, who defeated an enormous army with a mere three hundred men.

Significantly, Gideon's story began with a divine encounter. The angel of the Lord greeted him, saying, "The LORD is with you, mighty warrior," as though to say that God's mere presence would be enough to transform this fearful man into a mighty warrior capable of winning the peace for an entire nation.

Humbled by the encounter, Gideon built an altar, calling it "The LORD is Peace." What a statement! Israel had been bullied, fearful, and defeated. The land was ravaged. People were living in caves. Gideon himself, the "mighty warrior," had been hiding in a winepress when the angel of the Lord appeared to him. Yet the name of the altar was well considered. God was about to deliver his people and bring peace through a series of remarkable events. And he would use Gideon, the weakest man in the region, to bring about a peace that would last forty years—until Israel again fell away from God.

It's a great story, but what does it have to do with us? For one thing it reminds us that the peace we long for comes only from God. We need the reminder because we are so easily fooled into thinking that personal security lies elsewhere—in a fat retirement account, the perfect relationship, a good education, a prestigious job. And if we aren't careful, the blessings we crave may turn into desires that destroy our peace. Real peace comes only from practicing the presence of God.

If you have been feeling troubled and restless, harassed or oppressed, take a look inside. What's stealing your peace? What's making you anxious and frustrated? Have you slipped away from God? Have you become too busy to practice his presence and seek his face? Have you made compromises that have slowly eroded your faith? If the answer to any of these questions is yes, cry out to God as the people of Israel did in Gideon's day. Ask him to draw you more deeply into his presence, delivering you from the enemies of your soul intent on stealing your peace and robbing you of the good things he intends.

Wednesday

PRAYING THE NAME

Do not be anxious about anything, but in everything, by prayer and petition, with thanksgiving, present your requests to God. And the peace of God, which transcends all understanding, will guard your hearts and your minds in Christ Jesus. (Philippians 4:6–7)

Reflect On: Philippians 4:6–9
Praise God: Because he is full of mercy.
Offer Thanks: That God's Son is our peace.
Confess: Any habits of worry and anxiety.
Ask God: To grant you the peace that passes understanding.

My father was a man who loved to drink. He loved it better than his work, better than his wife, and better than any of his five children, though he wouldn't have put it that way. Most of the family believed he would die drinking. It was hard to imagine another outcome after forty years of a steady habit. But we were wrong.

Dad shocked us by admitting one day that he was an alcoholic, a man who had lost control of himself and was desperate for help. After he stopped drinking, he did his best to make up for the years of neglect and the broken relationships. And it was easy to see God's hand in all of it even though there was a residue of bitterness and anger in him that never quite healed.

Several years later, I sat by his bed as he lay in a coma, near death. His third-floor hospital room had a million-dollar view, though he never knew it. Through the window I could see a small lake shining in the afternoon sun, a white boat floating on its placid surface. I watched as the leaves of the trees bordering the lake rustled in the warm breeze. The picture was peaceful, serene—everything I wasn't.

Inside the hospital room my father's labored breathing formed the backdrop for my anxious prayers. I was reminding God of all the good things Dad had done in his life. He had fought courageously in World War II and had been a great friend and encourager to me in the latter years of his life. I knew that he had made huge efforts to stifle his many "Archie Bunkerisms" when he had begun living with me and my children three years earlier. His rakish humor had never deserted him even during the worst moments of his long illness. And he had never complained—not once.

As I thought of all these good things about my father, I pleaded for mercy regarding his shortcomings and the self-inflicted disappointments of his life. I was particularly aware of the unresolved anger that plagued him.

But as I prayed, I was startled by a different thought, one that took my prayers in a new direction. God seemed to be saying: "The good he has done just won't cut it." Strangely, I wasn't discouraged but buoyed up. How could I have forgotten one of the most basic tenets of my faith? I was praying as though my father had to purchase a ticket to heaven with the currency of his good deeds. But only the love of God and the mercy of Christ, I reminded myself, is powerful enough to bring any of us home safely.

Suddenly my father's failings seemed less worrisome, less relevant to the moment of his dying. I thought about the title of an old hymn, "There's a Wideness in God's Mercy," and the words comforted me. As I left that day, I realized the anxiety was gone. The peace I felt now seemed a perfect reflection of the tranquil scene outside his hospital window.

Two days later, just a few hours before my father died, I listened as this passage from the Bible was read during the Sunday service: "If God is for us, who can be against us? . . . Who will bring any charge against those whom God has chosen? It is God who justifies. Who is he that condemns?" (Romans 8:31, 33–34). The fear I had felt about my father's dying had evaporated. In its place was a steady peace.

What is it that is making you anxious today? Don't let it rob you of the peace God promises. Instead, entrust your situation to him in prayer. Ask him to guard your heart and your mind by giving you the peace that transcends all understanding.

Thursday

PRAYING THE NAME

Pray for the peace of Jerusalem:
"May those who love you be secure.
May there be peace within your walls
and security within your citadels."
For the sake of my brothers and friends,
I will say, "Peace be within you." (Psalm 122:6–8)

Reflect On: Psalm 122
Praise God: For his sovereignty over the nations and rulers of the world.
Offer Thanks: For the peace we have enjoyed as a nation.
Confess: Any lack of faith in God's power to bring peace.
Ask God: To create a lasting peace in the Middle East.

Several years ago, I spent a week in Jerusalem, touring the city, praying in its churches, and visiting its holy sites. Walking its ancient walls, one day, in sight of the Mount of Olives, I began to pray, asking God to bless the city with peace, as the psalmist instructs. As I prayed, Christians, Jews, and Muslims mingled in the densely packed streets below. I could hear men shouting, carrying on an endless argument about who knows what. The air was thick with fumes from the buses that rumbled along outside the wall. I found it hard to pray, hard to believe that this noisy, smelly, fascinating city would ever find peace, hard to believe that Jerusalem means "city of peace."

A few days earlier a Jewish man had been stabbed by a Muslim extremist as he walked through the butcher's market, his blood mingling with that of the animals slaughtered there. That week the Greek Orthodox Patriarch was injured in a riot while leading a procession near a house in the Old City that had been taken over by Jewish extremists. Their actions had set off a territorial dispute within the city. As I walked through the narrow streets shortly after the riot, I could smell tear gas mingled with incense.

Dissension, it seems, is a way of life in Jerusalem. And it isn't just Jews and Arabs who are at war. Ultraorthodox Jews fight with other Jews about regulations regarding food, dress, and Sabbath-keeping. Some Jewish women have been stoned and spit on because of how they dress. One woman, dressed in a short-sleeve shift cut above the knee, returned to her parked car to find the tires slashed, the doors covered with a film of eggs, and a flyer taped to a nearby wall proclaiming the message that "Parking in Immodest Dress Is Forbidden."

Unfortunately, some of Jerusalem's Christians are no better. At times the Israeli police have had to break up fistfights between monks from various sects arguing about the care and control of the Church of the Holy Sepulchre, one of Christendom's holiest shrines.

It's a mess, a shambles, a shame. What if Jesus were to walk through the streets of Jerusalem today? It's not hard to imagine him weeping over it as he did two thousand years ago.

But there are worse stories—far worse—such as the recent report of an Israeli helicopter firing five missiles into a car containing an Hamas official and his two bodyguards. All three of the bodies were burned and bloodied beyond recognition. Enraged by what they had just seen, a group of Palestinian men gathered around the vehicle, dunking their fists in the blood and soot and then raising them in the air, threatening revenge and chanting, "God is great."

We shake our heads at the madness, wondering where it will end and fearful because the problems of this region of the world have now become our problems, though we little understand them. Today as you read the news about the Middle East, do something more than simply shaking your head and turning the page. Take a moment to pray for the peace of Jerusalem and for the people who live there—Jewish, Muslim, and Christian. Plead with *Yahweh Shalom* that there will be a new openness to the gospel, the only true hope for peace. Try to make this prayer your habit whenever you listen to the news. And remember that peace in Jerusalem is what will make peace in the rest of the world possible.

Friday

Promises Associated with God's Name

To live in the presence of God through the power of the Holy Spirit is to be at peace—at peace with God, with others, with ourselves. He is the source of true *shalom,* of prosperity, harmony, safety, health, and fulfillment. No matter how turbulent our world becomes, we can be at peace, showing forth his presence regardless of circumstances.

Promises in Scripture

The fruit of the Spirit is love, joy, peace, patience, kindness, goodness, faithfulness, gentleness and self-control. Against such things there is no law. (Galatians 5:22)

Happy are those who find wisdom,
and those who get understanding. . . .
Her ways are ways of pleasantness,
and all her paths are peace. (Proverbs 3:13, 17 NRSV)

You will keep in perfect peace him whose mind is steadfast, because he trusts in you. (Isaiah 26:3)

"For I know the plans I have for you," declares the LORD, "plans to prosper you and not to harm you, plans to give you hope and a future. Then you will call upon me and come and pray to me, and I will listen to you. You will seek me and find me when you seek me with all your heart. I will be found by you," declares the LORD. (Jeremiah 29:11–14)

Continued Prayer and Praise

Pray this blessing over your family. (Numbers 6:22–27)

Pray for the peace of Jerusalem. (Isaiah 66:10–12)

Pray for the return of peace to your own life. (Lamentations 3:19–24)

Pray for the peace of Christ to rule in your heart. (Colossians 3:12–17)

13

The Lord of Hosts

Yahweh Tsebaoth

The Name

The Lord of Hosts is a title that emphasizes God's rule over every other power in the material and spiritual universe. When Scripture speaks of "the host of heaven," it is usually speaking of celestial bodies, though the phrase can also refer to angelic beings. The word "host" can also refer to human beings and to nature itself. When you pray to *Yahweh Tsebaoth,* you are praying to a God so magnificent that all creation serves his purposes.

Key Scripture

But David said to the Philistine, "You come to me with sword and spear and javelin; but I come to you in the name of the LORD of hosts, the God of the armies of Israel, whom you have defied. This very day the LORD will deliver you into my hand." (1 Samuel 17:45–46 NRSV)

Monday

God Reveals His Name

Saul clothed David with his armor; he put a bronze helmet on his head and clothed him with a coat of mail. David strapped Saul's sword over the armor, and he tried in vain to walk, for he was not used to them. Then David said to Saul, "I cannot walk with these; for I am not used to them." So David removed them. Then he took his staff in his hand, and chose five smooth stones from the wadi, and put them in his shepherd's bag, in the pouch; his sling was in his hand, and he drew near to the Philistine [Goliath].

The Philistine came on and drew near to David, with his shield bearer, in front of him. When the Philistine looked and saw David, he disdained him, for he was only a youth, ruddy and handsome in appearance. The Philistine said to David, "Am I a dog, that you come to me with sticks?" And the Philistine cursed David by his gods. The Philistine said to David, "Come to me, and I will give your flesh to the birds of the air and to the wild animals of the field." But David said to the Philistine, "You come to me with sword and spear and javelin; but I come to you in the name of the LORD of hosts, the God of the armies of Israel, whom you have defied. This very day the LORD will deliver you into my hand, and I will strike you down and cut off your head; and I will give the dead bodies of the Philistine army this very day to the birds of the air and to the wild animals of the earth, so that all the earth may know that there is a God in Israel, and that all this assembly may know that the LORD does not save by sword and spear; for the battle is the LORD's and he will give you into our hand." (1 Samuel 17:38–47 NRSV)

Lord God of Hosts, Yahweh Tsebaoth, help me to call upon your all-powerful name as I face challenges of various kinds. Take away my fear and arm me with faith and confidence. Use me to advance your kingdom in the midst of the struggles that lie ahead, and help me to remember that the battle always belongs to you. Amen.

Understanding the Name

Yahweh Tsebaoth (yah-WEH tse-ba-OATH) is a title of great power. It occurs more than 240 times in the Hebrew Scriptures, reminding us that all of creation, even in its fallen condition, is under God's rule and reign. At times Scripture speaks of the Lord of Hosts leading a great army. Cherubim and seraphim; sun and moon; stars and sky; rivers and mountains; hail and snow; men and women; animals, wild and tame—all these worship the Lord and are at times called to fight on his behalf. The NIV translates this title as "LORD Almighty."

Studying the Name

1. Why do you think the story emphasizes David's inability to do battle in the king's armor?
2. Contrast David's attitude toward the battle with Goliath's.
3. Remember times in your own life when you felt embattled. How did you deal with your struggles?
4. What one thing could you do today that would help you face future battles with greater faith?

Tuesday

Praying the Name

When the servant of the man of God got up and went out early the next morning, an army with horses and chariots had surrounded the city. "Oh, my lord, what shall we do?" the servant asked.

"Don't be afraid," the prophet answered. "Those who are with us are more than those who are with them."

And Elisha prayed, "O Lord, open his eyes so he may see." Then the Lord opened the servant's eyes, and he looked and saw the hills full of horses and chariots of fire all around Elisha. (2 Kings 6:15–17)

Reflect On: 2 Kings 6:8–23
Praise God: Because he is well able to help you.
Offer Thanks: For the specific ways God has helped you in the past.
Confess: Any lack of faith in God's desire or ability to help you.
Ask God: To open your eyes to his care.

I owe my love of reading to comic books, which I devoured by the hundreds as a child. Many of them sported ads picturing ninety-pound weaklings transformed into muscle-bound brutes after a few short weeks on a bodybuilding regimen. Even though I couldn't see myself as a weight lifter, I relished the idea of turning into the Incredible Hulk every once in a while. I could imagine the look of terror on my brother's face the next time he picked a fight with his little sister only to find her transformed into a superhuman fighting machine!

The closest I ever got to attaining Incredible Hulk status occurred late one summer night when I was a teenager lounging on the front porch of our home. The porch light was off and the street was dark, but I could see enough to make out two boys harassing a neighbor's miniature Schnauzer across the street. Malicious laughter mingled with the dog's pitiful yelps. Without thinking, I stood up and shouted out in my deepest, most authoritative voice, "Hey, you kids, leave that dog alone!" Unable to pinpoint the direction from which the terrifying voice had emanated, those boys took off so fast that I fell over laughing. It felt good to be powerful, especially on behalf of the innocent.

I wonder if that's how the prophet Elisha felt when he realized just who was fighting on his side against the king of Aram. Elisha had irritated that king by using his prophetic gifts to inform the king of Israel of the whereabouts of Aram's army. Furious, the king of Aram ordered his army to track him down.

When Elisha's servant awoke one morning and saw Aram's army surrounding the city in which they were staying, he panicked. But Elisha prayed, asking God to open his servant's eyes. The man was astonished when he looked out and saw a vast army of the heavenly host—horses and chariots of fire—surrounding the enemy.

That was good, but it gets better.

Next Elisha asked God to close the eyes of his enemies. Then he approached the soldiers, who were suddenly blinded, coolly informing them that they had made a slight miscalculation. They had surrounded the wrong city. But not to worry because he would rectify matters by leading them straight to the man they were looking for. Then Elisha marched them to Samaria, the capital of Israel. After that the prophet prayed a third time, asking God to open their eyes. Imagine the soldiers' surprise at finding themselves captives in the heart of enemy territory.

No wonder the psalmist says that "he who sits in the heavens laughs" at all the kings of the earth. Perhaps in this case, Elisha, the wiliest of prophets, fell over laughing too.

This story reminds us of an important reality: No matter who is against us, God is for us. The next time you feel like panicking, besieged by an army of troubles, cry out to the Lord of Hosts for his help. Ask him to open your eyes to the way he is already working on your behalf. Remember the words of Elisha: "Those who are with us are more than those who are with them."

Wednesday

PRAYING THE NAME

The nations are in an uproar, the kingdoms totter;
he utters his voice, the earth melts.
The LORD *of hosts is with us;*
the God of Jacob is our refuge. (Psalm 46:6–7 NRSV*)*

Reflect On: Psalm 46
Praise God: Who is exalted among the nations.
Offer Thanks: That God defends his people.
Confess: Any tendency to reject God's love for you.
Ask God: To strengthen you in the midst of spiritual battles.

In 1529 Martin Luther, the famous reformer, wrote a hymn that has proven popular through the centuries. Included in the National Service of Prayer and Remembrance held shortly after the September 11, 2001, terrorist attack on the World Trade Center in New York, it celebrates the power of this wonderful name of God. Known to the world as "A Mighty Fortress Is Our God," the second verse of the hymn goes like this:

Did we in our own strength confide, our striving would
be losing;
Were not the right man on our side, the man of God's
own choosing.
Dost ask who that may be? Christ Jesus, it is he;
Lord Sabaoth his name, from age to age the same,
And he must win the battle.

Luther, with countless battles of his own to fight, was celebrating the fact that *Yahweh Tsebaoth,* the Lord of Hosts, would triumph over whatever devils might face us in this world. The words of his memorable hymn are based to some extent on Psalm 46.

G. Campbell Morgan, pastor of Westminster Chapel in London during the early part of the twentieth century, points out something rather remarkable about verse 7 of this psalm. The Lord of Hosts—the God of sun and moon, people and angels, the great and terrible God whose army is comprised of the entire created world—is in the same breath called "the God of Jacob"—the God of a single, solitary human being whose life was anything but perfect. Here's how Campbell Morgan puts it:

> I know only one man who is meaner than Jacob and that is Laban. The only comfort I ever got out of Jacob is that he was one too many for Laban. Of all men for astute, hard-driving meanness recommend me to Jacob. But God is "the God of Jacob." . . . Oh, my soul, here find thy comfort! I do not know whether it helps you, but it helps me. He is the God of Jacob, mean as Jacob was. This is the thing on which my faith fastens. "The Lord of hosts . . ." yes; but "the God of Jacob!". . . But was that man such a man as I? The longer I live the more astonished I am that God ever loved me at all. The longer I live the more astonished I am at that infinite grace which found me and loves me and keeps me. The meanness that lurks within, the possibilities of evil that I have discovered make me ask, "Will God look at me?" He is "the God of Jacob."

Later, Campbell Morgan adds this: "It is not only in immensity but in littleness that God is great." God shows himself great not only in shaping the universe to his design but in reshaping our small hearts to accomplish his large purposes. The Lord of Hosts—the God of Jacob: He is our God too!

Thursday

PRAYING THE NAME

For a child has been born for us,
a son given to us:
authority rests upon his shoulders. . . .
His authority shall grow continually,
and there shall be endless peace
for the throne of David and his kingdom.
He will establish and uphold it
with justice and with righteousness
from this time onward and forevermore.
The zeal of the LORD of hosts will do this.
(Isaiah 9:6–7 NRSV)

Reflect On:	Isaiah 9:6–7
Praise God:	For his plan of salvation.
Offer Thanks:	Because you belong to the Lord of Hosts.
Confess:	Any complacency about your faith.
Ask God:	To equip you for the spiritual battles that will surely come.

Recent wars in Afghanistan and Iraq have displayed in terrifying detail the power of high tech weaponry. Smart bombs, cluster bombs, bunker bombs—we've devised ingenious new ways to win battles. But even the most sophisticated weaponry in the history of the world is nothing next to God, who has at his disposal the entire created universe with which to accomplish his purposes. Consider a few of the memorable stories in Scripture that portray creation fighting on behalf of *Yahweh Tsebaoth,* the Lord of Hosts:

- Locusts swarming over Egypt (Exodus 10:12–15)
- The Red Sea parting (Exodus 14:15–31)
- The earth swallowing up the guilty (Numbers 16:28–35)
- The sun locked in its place until a battle is won (Joshua 10:12–14)
- Thunder routing an enemy (1 Samuel 7:10–12)
- Fire consuming God's enemies but preserving his friends (Daniel 3:19–30)
- Lions cozying up to the prophet Daniel (Daniel 6:16–23)

Isaiah tells the story of how a single angel slew 185,000 Assyrian soldiers. Jesus, the night he was arrested, assured his disciples that he had more than six legions of such angels (72,000) at his beck and call!

With such clear evidence of God's power, couldn't the same man who cast out devils, walked on water, raised the dead, multiplied bread for thousands, and calmed a furious storm, have done something else to save himself, to save us?

We know the answer. It's a familiar story—hailed as both the high and low point of human history. It's the day God laid down his weapons and tied his hands behind his back—the day he let Satan have his way. His Son was whipped and mocked, stripped naked on a cross, cut with a crown of thorns pressed hard into his brow, and then publicly displayed, as though the devil's own trophy. But not for long. For this was the costliest of struggles, the greatest of prizes. Jesus became the Savior of the world, not through a display of supernatural power but through a display of apparent weakness. He discarded every weapon but his own perfect submission to his Father's will, laying down his life in a display of perfect faith, lowliness, and love.

Paul reminds us that our own struggle is not against flesh and blood "but against the rulers, against the authorities, against the powers of this dark world and against the spiritual forces of evil in the heavenly realms." And he urges us to come dressed for battle, to put on the full armor of God so that we can stand in the day of evil (Ephesians 6:12–13). As we stand, we are also to remember, that, despite appearances, when the battle is at its worst, the Lord of Hosts is still with us, "able to do immeasurably more than all we ask or imagine, according to his power that is at work within us" (Ephesians 3:20).

Friday

PROMISES ASSOCIATED WITH GOD'S NAME

What are you afraid of? Your children straying? Your marriage breaking up? Are you afraid of loneliness, sickness, financial trouble, failure, accidents, old age, death? Perhaps you worry that you will never find a life partner. Or maybe you are afraid God doesn't love you, that he can't forgive you, that he finds the essential you unacceptable. To be human is to be vulnerable, to be aware of limitations, weaknesses, and defects that may lead to our undoing. What's more, Satan plays on these weaknesses, accusing us day and night. In the spiritual struggle in which all of us are engaged, we need to stop giving him sway by listening to his lies. We need instead to accept the clear evidence of God's love for us, remembering always that the battle belongs to the Lord.

Promises in Scripture

"Be still, and know that I am God!
I am exalted among the nations,
I am exalted in the earth."
The LORD of hosts is with us;
the God of Jacob is our refuge. (Psalm 46:10–11 NRSV)

O LORD of hosts,
happy is everyone who trusts in you. (Psalm 84:12 NRSV)

Return to me, says the LORD of hosts, and I will return to you, says the LORD of hosts. (Zechariah 1:3 NRSV)

Then those who revered the LORD spoke with one another. The LORD took note and listened, and a book of remembrance was written before him of those who revered the LORD and thought on his name. They shall be mine, says the L*ORD of hosts, my special possession on the day when I act, and I will spare them as parents spare their children who serve them. (Malachi 3:16–17* NRSV*)*

Continued Prayer and Praise

Remember that no one can thwart the plans of the Lord of Hosts. (Isaiah 14:24–27)

Pray for restoration. (Psalm 80:19)

Let all creation praise the Lord of Hosts. (Psalm 148)

14

The Lord My Rock

יהוה צוּרִי

Yahweh Tsuri

The Name

What better word than "rock" to represent God's permanence, protection, and enduring faithfulness? When you pray to the Lord your Rock, you are praying to the God who can always be counted on. His purposes and plans remain firm throughout history. The New Testament identifies Jesus as the spiritual rock that accompanied the Israelites during their long journey through the desert. He is also the stone the builders rejected but that has become the cornerstone of God's church.

Key Scripture

Praise be to the LORD my Rock,
  who trains my hands for war
  my fingers for battle. (Psalm 144:1)

Monday

GOD REVEALS HIS NAME

Praise be to the LORD my Rock,
    who trains my hands for war
    my fingers for battle.
He is my loving God and my fortress,
    my stronghold and my deliverer....
Reach down your hand from on high;
    deliver me and rescue me
from the mighty waters,
    from the hands of foreigners
whose mouths are full of lies,
    whose right hands are deceitful.
I will sing a new song to you, O God;
    on the ten-stringed lyre I will make music to you,
to the One who gives victory to kings,
    who delivers his servant David from the deadly
        sword. (Psalm 144:1–2, 7–10)

Lord, you are more reliable than the ground I stand on and your faithfulness is more than I can comprehend. Thank you for hearing my voice and rescuing me when I cry to you. When I am shaken, you steady me. When I am in trouble, you save me. Amen.

Understanding the Name

Rocks provided shade, shelter, and safety in the wilderness and were used to construct altars, temples, houses, and city walls. Heaps of stones were also used to commemorate important events in Israel's history. God's commandments, given to Moses, were etched on stone so that all generations would learn his law. The word "rock" epitomizes his enduring faithfulness. The Hebrew noun *tsur* is often translated "rock" or "stone," while *petra* is the Greek word for rock. To worship *Yahweh Tsuri* (yah-WEH tsu-REE) is to echo Hannah's great prayer of praise: "There is no Rock like our God" (1 Samuel 2:2).

Studying the Name

1. David praised God for delivering him from his enemies. What kind of enemies do you face or have you faced in the past? How have you dealt with them?
2. David expressed his sense of vulnerability with vivid images. Describe a time in your life when you felt particularly vulnerable?
3. How has God heard your cries for help?
4. How would your life be different if you experienced more deeply the truth that God is your Rock?

Tuesday

PRAYING THE NAME

He [David] said:

> *"The LORD is my rock, my fortress and my deliverer,*
> *my God is my rock, in whom I take refuge,*
> *my shield and the horn of my salvation.*
> *He is my stronghold, my refuge and my savior—*
> *from violent men you save me.*
> *I call to the LORD, who is worthy of praise,*
> *and I am saved from my enemies. (2 Samuel 22:2–4)*

Reflect On:	1 Samuel 24:1–13 and 2 Samuel 22:2–4
Praise God:	For being your rock.
Offer Thanks:	For the way God has delivered you from enemies.
Confess:	Any times in which you have retaliated against others.
Ask God:	To give you the humility not to strike back when someone offends you.

After dropping my children at school one morning, I stopped at the grocery store to pick up a few things. On my way out of the parking lot a driver in another car beeped at me, mistakenly thinking he had the right of way. Being a good Christian, I turned the other cheek and let him pass, right? Of course not! I kept on going, heading straight out in front of him. Then he beeped again. Tired of ignoring his boorish behavior, I gave him a backward beep (since I was already in front of him), proceeded smugly into traffic, and began muttering to myself about the low I.Q. of the Neanderthal behind me.

Then I read this passage and was struck with the contrast between my response to this man, whose offense was small, and David's response to a man whose offense was great.

You may remember that King Saul made himself David's enemy by repeatedly trying to murder him. Surprisingly, though David defended himself, he refused to retaliate even when he had the perfect opportunity. One time Saul and his army were chasing David, when Saul entered a cave to relieve himself. He had no idea that David was hiding inside. Talk about a sitting duck! David could have set things straight in an instant and no one would have blamed him. But instead of killing Saul, David merely crept up behind him and sliced off a piece of his robe as evidence that he intended the king no harm.

Few of us have enemies with a big "E" as David did. Most of ours are the small "e" variety, like drivers who try to cut us off, teachers who dislike our children, insurance companies that refuse to pay claims, coworkers who speak ill of us. David had the grace to respond to his enemy with mercy because he knew that God himself would deal with Saul. He had no need to get even. No need to vindicate himself. No need to strike out. He believed that the promises God had made were as solid as the rock he stood on. And in the end, God took care of things, punishing Saul but not by David's hand. When David finally became king, he took the throne without having Saul's blood on his hands.

We, too, will have our battles, though they may not be as dramatic as David's. Like him, we can respond with humility and trust, defending ourselves without giving in to our desire to retaliate, confident that the God whom David called his Rock—the One who is true to every promise—is the same God who is with us.

Wednesday

PRAYING THE NAME

Those who trust in the LORD are like Mount Zion,
which cannot be shaken but endures forever.
As the mountains surround Jerusalem,
so the LORD surrounds his people
both now and forevermore. (Psalm 125:1–2)

Reflect On: Psalm 125:1–2
Praise God: For his reliability and fidelity.
Offer Thanks: For the ways God has steadied you in fearful times.
Confess: Your tendency to trust in circumstances rather than in God.
Ask God: To help you exchange your fear for his peace.

As I write, the skies are a sullen gray, threatening snow. Several days of rain have stripped all but the most stubborn trees, readying them for winter's onslaught. This is Grand Rapids, a city in southwestern Michigan that has weather the opposite of Tucson, Arizona, a 360-sunny-days-a-year kind of town, with majestic mountains surrounding it like the encircling arms of God. But it wasn't until I moved from Tucson to Grand Rapids, a city encircled not by mountains but by clouds, that the psalmist's words came home to me.

Each week I join with a handful of women committed to supporting each other spiritually. A few years ago, one of them asked for prayers for her college-bound son. We asked God to supply the best school for him. Our prayers were dogged. We prayed for several months, through various applications and school visits until the best school finally emerged—an exclusive college with an unusual approach to tuition. Every admitted student received a full-tuition scholarship. The catch was getting admitted. Though Nick had only the slimmest chance, we kept on praying. When the acceptance letter arrived, Sandy was ecstatic, and we were heartened by this obvious answer to prayer.

At the end of the summer of 2001, my friend dropped her son off in downtown Manhattan to attend Cooper Union. Sandy had been glad that this college would offer Nick a larger window on the world, never dreaming just how large that window would become. It wasn't long after the term started when Nick looked out his dorm window and saw smoke billowing from the collapse of the World Trade Center's Twin Towers. Nick's school was less than two miles from the site of what has become the worst terrorist attack in American history.

In the days and weeks that followed, I watched my friend for signs of hysteria. But there were none. While other parents were making knee-jerk comments about withdrawing their children from colleges in exotic locations like Iowa and Indiana, anxious to have them close, Sandy felt fine about Nick staying put in Manhattan. It would have been easy to give in to the contagion of fear that characterized the country at that time. Nobody would have blamed her if she had tried to haul her son home. But Sandy didn't even seem tempted. Believing that God had led Nick to New York for a purpose gave her the kind of peace that only God can create.

Watching my friend respond to terror with trust has convinced me that whether we live in New York, Grand Rapids, Tucson, or lands beyond, it is still true that the Lord surrounds his people. He encircles us with his faithfulness just as the mountains surround Jerusalem.

Thursday

Praying the Name

Therefore everyone who hears these words of mine and puts them into practice is like a wise man who built his house on the rock. The rain came down, the streams rose, and the winds blew and beat against that house; yet it did not fall because it had its foundation on the rock. (Matthew 7:24–25)

For in Scripture it says:

"See, I lay a stone in Zion,
a chosen and precious cornerstone,
and the one who trusts in him
will never be put to shame." (1 Peter 2:6)

Reflect On: Matthew 7:24–27
Praise God: For his unshakable faithfulness.
Offer Thanks: For the security we have in Christ.
Confess: Any habit of worry that keeps you from trusting God.
Ask God: To help you put his words into practice.

A few years ago a friend told me the story of a dream his twelve-year-old son, Christopher, had been having—a nightmare that recurred several times during a monthlong period. Whenever the boy focused on an object in his dream, it would suddenly shrink and then start spinning counterclockwise at ever-increasing speeds. The experience was so unnerving that when he woke up, he saw objects in his bedroom growing smaller and smaller and then beginning to spin uncontrollably, just like in his nightmare. Finally one night the dream changed.

"I was having the dream," Christopher explained, "when suddenly a slab of stone appeared right in front of my face so I couldn't see anything else. It looked like it was some kind of marble and had handles on either side and writing on it. As soon as I saw it, I grabbed on to the handles. When I looked closer, I realized the inscription read: 'Jesus Is the Rock.' It blocked out all the stuff that had been scaring me, and I never had the dream again."

Christopher's dream offers a wonderful image of how Jesus can deal with our fear. When Christopher was looking at the stone, he couldn't see anything else, not even the things that frightened him. Grabbing hold of the rock, he was at peace and the nightmare vanished.

What are you facing today that frightens you or shakes your confidence? Illness? Job loss? Trouble at home? Difficulties at work? No matter how out of control life may seem, decide to keep your eyes glued to Jesus—to his character and his faithfulness and not to the circumstances that disturb you. Recommit yourself not only to hearing his Word but to building your life on it, confident that when the rains come down, the streams rise up, and the winds blow and beat against your house, it will not fall because its foundation is securely built on the rock.

Friday

PROMISES ASSOCIATED WITH GOD'S NAME

Perfect peace, rest, unshakable faith, salvation—these enduring promises belong to all who trust in God. These blessings come, not by wishing but by willing, by deciding to sink our roots into God, spending time in prayer, reading his Word, holding fast to his commandments, and yielding to his Spirit at work within us. Scripture tells us we are to live and move and have our being in the God who made us. When tragedy comes, as it inevitably will, and when the world around us begins to tremble and shake, as it inevitably will, we will not be shaken. Instead, the Lord who is the Rock eternal will be there, giving us rest and peace.

Promises in Scripture

You will keep in perfect peace him
whose mind is steadfast,
because he trusts in you.
Trust in the LORD forever,
for the LORD, the LORD, is the Rock eternal. (Isaiah 26:3–4)

My soul finds rest in God alone;
my salvation comes from him.
He alone is my rock and my salvation;
he is my fortress, I will never be shaken. (Psalm 62:1–2)

Come, let us sing for joy to the LORD;
let us shout aloud to the Rock of our salvation. (Psalm 95:1)

Continued Prayer and Praise

Find a way to commemorate what God has done for you. (1 Samuel 7:10)

Remember that Jesus was the spiritual rock that accompanied God's people in the desert. (Exodus 17:1–6; 1 Corinthians 10:1–5)

Begin to see yourself as a living stone with Christ as the cornerstone. (1 Peter 2:4–8)

15

THE LORD IS MY SHEPHERD

יהוה רֹעִי

YAHWEH ROI

The Name

For at least part of their history, the Hebrews were a nomadic people who wandered from place to place seeking pasture for their herds of sheep, goats, and cattle. To sustain their livelihood, it was vital for shepherds to keep their animals from straying, protect them from thieves and wild animals, and provide them with plentiful pastures. In the ancient Near East and in Israel itself, "shepherd" eventually became a metaphor for kings. The Hebrew Scriptures speak of God as the Shepherd of his people and apply this image to religious leaders as well. The New Testament presents Jesus as the Good Shepherd, who protects the lives of his sheep by forfeiting his own life. When you pray to the Lord your Shepherd, you are praying to the One who watches over you day and night, feeding you and leading you safely on the path of righteousness.

Key Scripture

The LORD is my shepherd, I shall not be in want.
    He makes me lie down in green pastures,
he leads me beside quiet waters,
    he restores my soul.
He guides me in paths of righteousness
    for his name's sake. (Psalm 23:1–3)

Monday

GOD REVEALS HIS NAME

The LORD is my shepherd, I shall not be in want.
    He makes me lie down in green pastures,
he leads me beside quiet waters,
    he restores my soul.
He guides me in paths of righteousness
    for his name's sake.
Even though I walk
    through the valley of the shadow of death,
I will fear no evil,
    for you are with me;
your rod and your staff,
    they comfort me.
You prepare a table before me
    in the presence of my enemies.
You anoint my head with oil;
    my cup overflows.
Surely goodness and love will follow me
    all the days of my life,
and I will dwell in the house of the LORD
    forever. (Psalm 23)

Lord, I praise you for your constant care—for bringing me back when I have wandered from your ways; for nourishing me, body and soul; for protecting me in the dark times; for making me lie down in peace. Because you are my Shepherd, I will fear no evil. Every day of my life will be filled with your goodness and love. Amen.

Understanding the Name

Shepherding was one of the earliest human occupations. A family's wealth was measured by how many sheep, goats, cows, horses, camels, and/or asses a man owned. Abel, Abraham, Isaac, Jacob, Moses, and David were all shepherds. Before David fought Goliath, he told Saul: "Your servant has been keeping his father's sheep. When a lion or a bear came and carried off a sheep from the flock, I went after it, struck it and rescued the sheep from its mouth. When it turned on me, I seized it by its hair, struck it and killed it" (1 Samuel 17:34–35).

It was the shepherd's responsibility to count each animal to order to make sure none had gone astray. At night, sheep were kept in simple enclosures, in caves or within walls made from bushes. At times, the shepherd would sleep with his body lying across the gate to the enclosure in order to keep the sheep safe. Though Israel's religious leaders were also referred to as shepherds, they were often chided for their failure to watch over the flock of God. Both then and now *Yahweh Roi* (yah-WEH row-EE) is the one true Shepherd of his people.

Studying the Name

1. Read the first three sentences of this familiar psalm slowly, then close your eyes. Imagine that you are the sheep. What do you see? What do you feel?
2. What does it mean to "restore the soul"? Describe a time when you felt in need of such a restoration.
3. Read the fourth sentence slowly. Imagine again that you are the sheep. What do you see? What do you feel?
4. Why do you think the psalmist introduces the imagery of a table?
5. How would your experience of daily life change if you really believed that goodness and kindness would follow you all the days of your life?

Tuesday

PRAYING THE NAME

Even though I walk
through the valley of the shadow of death,
I will fear no evil,
for you are with me;
your rod and your staff,
they comfort me. (Psalm 23:4)

Reflect On: Psalm 23
Praise God: For his ability to care for you.
Offer Thanks: For the way God has been your faithful Shepherd.
Confess: Any tendency to let fear shape your responses to life.
Ask God: To restore your soul and give you peace.

According to scientists, sheep have gotten a bad reputation for being, shall we say, less than brilliant. In fact, it appears that sheep are fairly intelligent creatures. They only seem stupid because they are afraid of just about everything. But what's so scary about being a sheep? For one thing sheep taste good, especially to wolves and other wild animals who love to prey on them because they are defenseless. To make matters worse, sheep are fairly good at getting lost, and when they get wet in a river or pond, their wool can get so soaked and heavy that they easily drown. Close to shearing time sheep can become so top-heavy that they may fall over and not be able to get up, making them easy targets for predator birds. Sheep, it seems, are a tragedy waiting to happen. It's little wonder that their sense of vulnerability sometimes leads to panic and wooly-brained behavior.

Though we rarely like to admit it, we too are subject to fears that sometimes cause us to behave stupidly. Afraid of failing in business, we're tempted to cut corners. Frightened by loneliness, we fall prey to relationships that harm us emotionally and spiritually. Fearful that we're going to miss out, we spend money foolishly. Worried that something terrible will happen to our children, we try vainly to control their lives. Fear can become so powerful that it pushes us off the path of righteousness, making us more vulnerable to various kinds of evil. Oddly, some of us are even afraid to admit how fearful we are. Yet fear shapes our behaviors and choices in ways that lead not to greater security but to deepened anxiety.

No wonder we need a Shepherd to keep us safe, to guide us along the right path, and to lead us through the valley of the shadow of death. Today, ask the Lord to examine your heart, training a spotlight on your fears. As each one is revealed, ask him to help you conquer it through faith. Pray that God will replace your fear with a sense of security so strong that you can say with the psalmist, "The Lord is my Shepherd. . . . I fear no evil."

Wednesday

PRAYING THE NAME

We all, like sheep, have gone astray,
each of us has turned to his own way;
and the LORD *has laid on him*
the iniquity of us all. (Isaiah 53:6–7)

For the Lamb at the center of the throne will be their shepherd;
he will lead them to springs of living water.
(Revelation 7:17)

Reflect On:	Isaiah 53
Praise God:	For his mercy in calling us back to himself.
Offer Thanks:	That God gave his only Son to be both the Lamb who laid down his life for us and the Shepherd who brings us home.
Confess:	Any tendency to depart from God's ways.
Ask God:	To help you keep your eyes on him so that you will not stray.

An absent-minded professor I know of once stood beside his car in a college parking lot looking perplexed. When one of his students walked by, he caught his arm and asked, "Excuse me, I wonder if you could tell me? Am I coming or going?"

A friend of mine once misplaced his car for a full week. It seems he had parked it in front of a store, walked off to do some errands, and then walked a short distance home, completely forgetting that he had driven to the store in the first place. The next day, he was surprised to find that the car wasn't in the garage, and he couldn't remember where he had put it!

Another directionally challenged friend has a habit, whenever she has forgotten where she has parked, of pushing the panic button on a remote keyless entry device to locate her car. It's not a subtle method, but flashing headlights and beeping horns work for her.

We chuckle at such stories, but Scripture reminds us that without Christ we are all directionally challenged, incapable of living a life that's spiritually on course, and vulnerable to a world of troubles. Like sheep who have gone astray, we are pulled off the path by our disordered desires, our selfish natures, and our attraction to sin. We are like rebellious toddlers who break free from their mother and start running toward traffic, heedless of danger.

Today, reflect on the fact that Jesus is called both the Lamb of God and the Good Shepherd. Thank him for becoming part of the flock, laying down his life so that we might have true life. Take some time to worship him and to recommit your life to him. Then pray for a child, a family member, a friend, or a business associate who seems far from God. Ask the Lord to search out that one lost sheep. Tell him you won't stop praying until he brings him back.

Thursday

Praying the Name

See, the Sovereign Lord comes with power,
and his arm rules for him.
See, his reward is with him,
and his recompense accompanies him.
He tends his flock like a shepherd:
He gathers the lambs in his arms
and carries them close to his heart;
he gently leads those that have young.
(Isaiah 40:10–11)

Reflect On: Isaiah 40:6–11
Praise God: Because he is gentle.
Offer Thanks: That God carries you close to his heart.
Confess: Any stubbornness that makes it difficult for God to lead you.
Ask God: To help you see your need for a Shepherd.

Isaiah presents an appealing image of our heavenly Shepherd. He is not only strong but also tender. He is able to defend us against any kind of danger or difficulty. Yet gathering the lambs in his arms, he gently leads the ewes. He is aware of our weakness and vulnerability and knows exactly who we are.

But do we? Though it's nice to think we have a heavenly Shepherd watching over us, it's hardly flattering to be compared to sheep. A. B. "Banjo" Paterson was a famous Australian writer who wrote about life in the Australian outback and whose credits include *The Man from Snowy River* and the lyrics for "Waltzing Mathilda." His laughable description of merino sheep should give us pause as we think about the task of shepherding, this time from God's perspective.

> People have got the impression that the merino is a gentle, bleating animal that gets its living without trouble to anybody, and comes up every year to be shorn with a pleased smile upon its amiable face. It is my purpose here to exhibit the merino sheep in its true light.
>
> The truth is that he is a dangerous monomaniac, and his one idea is to ruin the man who owns him. With this object in view he will display a talent for getting into trouble and a genius for dying that are almost incredible.
>
> If a mob of sheep see a bush fire closing round them, do they run away out of danger? Not at all, they rush round and round in a ring till the fire burns them up. If they are in a river-bed, with a howling flood coming down, they will stubbornly refuse to cross three inches of water to save themselves. Dogs may bark and men may shriek, but the sheep won't move. They will wait there till the flood comes and drowns them all, and then their corpses go down the river on their backs with their feet in the air.
>
> A mob will crawl along a road slowly enough to exasperate a snail, but let a lamb get away in a bit of rough country, and a race horse can't head him back again. . . .
>
> There is a well authenticated story of a ship-load of sheep that was lost because an old ram jumped overboard, and all the rest followed him. No doubt they did, and were proud to do it. A sheep won't go through an open gate on his own responsibility, but he would gladly and proudly "follow the leader" through the red-hot portals of Hades: and it makes no difference whether the lead goes voluntarily, or is hauled struggling and kicking and fighting every inch of the way.

Furthermore, Paterson says, "The fiendish resemblance which one sheep bears to another is a great advantage to them in their struggles with their owners. It makes it more difficult to draft them out of a strange flock, and much harder to tell when any are missing." And when it comes to rounding them up, he concludes: "Any man who has tried to drive rams on a hot day knows what purgatory is."

Sound familiar? Even a little bit? A talent for getting into trouble, stubborn, capable of great stupidity? Paterson's humorous remarks about merino sheep remind me, I'm sorry to say, of someone I know fairly well. What can I say but Baaaa!

Take a moment to laugh at yourself and to thank your heavenly Shepherd for being patient with you and your fellow sheep. The next time you're tempted to critique God's management of the universe, reread Banjo Paterson's description and see if that doesn't put everything back into perspective.

Friday

PROMISES ASSOCIATED WITH GOD'S NAME

When a herd grows to a hundred or more sheep in the Middle East, its owner can often afford to hire a shepherd to watch over them. God himself had appointed shepherds to guide his people, but many of them acted like hirelings, abandoning the sheep at the first sign of danger or even leading them astray for their own selfish motives. The same is true today whenever church leaders abandon the gospel in favor of money, power, or the pursuit of pleasure. Not only does God promise to judge such false and faithless shepherds, but he promises to shepherd his people himself. That promise is fulfilled in the life and ministry of Jesus, the one who is the Good Shepherd who lays down his life for his sheep.

Promises in Scripture

I myself will tend my sheep and have them lie down, declares the Sovereign LORD. I will search for the lost and bring back the strays. I will bind up the injured and strengthen the weak, but the sleek and the strong I will destroy. I will shepherd the flock with justice. (Ezekiel 34:15–16)

I am the good shepherd; I know my sheep and my sheep know me—just as the Father knows me and I know the Father—and I lay down my life for the sheep. I have other sheep that are not of this sheep pen. I must bring them also. They too will listen to my voice, and there shall be one flock and one shepherd. (John 10:14–18)

Continued Prayer and Praise

Pray that God will bring back the lost. (Ezekiel 34)

Remember that Jesus is the gate for the sheep. (John 10:7–10)

Praise Jesus, the shepherd who will wipe away every tear from our eyes. (Revelation 7:15–17)

16

The Name

Hashem

The Name

Shem is the Hebrew word for "name" (the "*Ha*" before it is the definite article). The Bible speaks of Solomon's temple in Jerusalem as the place where God's name would dwell—the place where his people could pray and be heard. Jesus himself prayed that the Father would glorify his name through him. He also promised to do whatever we ask in his name. Philippians 2:9–10 affirms that God has exalted Jesus and given him "the name that is above every name."

Key Scripture

Hear the cry and the prayer that your servant is praying in your presence this day. May your eyes be open toward this temple night and day, this place of which you said, "My Name shall be there," so that you will hear the prayer your servant prays toward this place. (1 Kings 8:28–29)

Monday

GOD REVEALS HIS NAME

Then Solomon stood before the altar of the LORD in front of the whole assembly of Israel, spread out his hands toward heaven and said ... "Hear the cry and the prayer that your servant is praying in your presence this day. May your eyes be open toward this temple night and day, this place of which you said, 'My Name shall be there,' so that you will hear the prayer your servant prays toward this place. Hear the supplication of your servant and of your people Israel when they pray toward this place. Hear from heaven, your dwelling place, and when you hear, forgive....

"When the heavens are shut up and there is no rain because your people have sinned against you, and when they pray toward this place and confess your name and turn from their sin because you have afflicted them, then hear from heaven and forgive the sin of your servants, your people Israel. Teach them the right way to live, and send rain on the land you gave your people for an inheritance....

"As for the foreigner who does not belong to your people Israel but has come from a distant land because of your name—for men will hear of your great name and your mighty hand and your outstretched arm—when he comes and prays toward this temple, then hear from heaven, your dwelling place, and do whatever the foreigner asks of you, so that all the peoples of the earth may know your name and fear you, as do your own people Israel, and may know that this house I have built bears your Name...."

When Solomon had finished building the temple of the LORD and the royal palace, and had achieved all he had desired to do ... the LORD said to him:

"I have heard the prayer and plea you have made before me; I have consecrated this temple, which you have built, by putting my Name there forever. My eyes and my heart will always be there." (From 1 Kings 8:22–9:3)

Lord, teach me what it means to "hallow your name," to glorify, exalt, declare, and praise your holy name, to live in a way that honors your name so that others might find forgiveness, peace, and healing through the power of your name. Amen.

Understanding the Name

God's name is associated with his glory, power, holiness, protection, trust, and love. To call on his name is to call on his presence. To act in his name is to act with his authority. To fight in his name is to fight with his power. To pray to his name is to pray to him. In fact, the very first mention of prayer in the Bible appears in Genesis 4:26: "At that time people began to invoke the name of the LORD" (NRSV). Though we are to exalt God's name and proclaim it to the nations, it is also possible to dishonor it, which is the same as dishonoring him. God's name is his reputation.

Though God's name is holy and powerful, it cannot be invoked as a magic formula. Rather, his name becomes powerful whenever it is uttered by men and women who are exercising their faith in God.

Jesus taught his own disciples to pray by saying, "Our Father who art in heaven, *hallowed be thy name*. . . ." In John's gospel, Jesus prays to his Father, saying, "I have manifested thy *name* to the men whom thou gavest me" and "I made known to them thy *name*, and I will make it known" (John 17:6, 26 KJV).

When we pray to *Hashem* (ha-SHAME), we are praying to the holy God who dwells in our midst, hearing and answering our prayers.

Studying the Name

1. What does it mean to confess God's name? What is the connection between repentance and answered prayer? (see 1 Kings 8:35–36)
2. Why do you think Solomon prayed that God would hear the prayers of foreigners when they prayed toward the temple? (see 1 Kings 8:41–43)

3. How can Solomon's great prayer at the dedication of the temple in Jerusalem inform your prayers today?
4. What does God mean when he says he will put his "Name" in the temple?
5. How have you experienced God's response to your own prayers?

Tuesday

PRAYING THE NAME

The Lord said to him [Solomon]: "I have heard the prayer and plea you have made before me; I have consecrated this temple, which you have built, by putting my Name there forever. My eyes and my heart will always be there." (1 Kings 9:3)

Reflect On: 1 Kings 8:1–11, 22–66; 9:1–3
Praise God: For his holy and powerful name.
Offer Thanks: Because God has promised to hear your prayers.
Confess: Any tendency to forget that you are a "temple of the living God."
Ask God: To increase your reverence for God's holy name.

My daughters were both born in China. When I adopted them as infants, I had the option of changing their names, which I did. For good measure I chose a Chinese middle name for each. But why change their names at all? For one thing, the girls had been named by orphanage personnel, not by their birth parents. In fact, all the children in their respective orphanages had exactly the same surname. So it hardly seemed like a distinctive, even though one of my children was named after the mayor of her city. I wanted their names to link them to our family and our future together, not to an institution.

In most societies parents have the right to name their children, even if this right seems at times to be abused. Believe it or not there are children in our world named "Gouda," "Veal," "Bologna," "Vanity," "Unique," "ESPN," "Gator," "Adonis," "Denim," and even "Dung." The list of strange names maintained by the Social Security Administration appears to be growing longer and stranger each year. Regardless of what we name our kids, naming is our prerogative as parents. By naming our children we are extending our authority over them, claiming them as our own, pledging our care and protection, and promising our lifelong commitment and love.

And that's what God did with his people. First, he revealed his name to his chosen people and then he associated his name and his presence with the temple that Solomon built in Jerusalem. By doing so, he promised to dwell with his people, hearing and answering their prayers as long as they remained faithful to him. Though the temple in Jerusalem is no longer standing, Paul reminds us that "we are the temple of the living God. As God has said: 'I will live with them and walk among them, and I will be their God, and they will be my people'" (2 Corinthians 6:16).

Since the first century, those who follow Jesus have been known as "Christians," named after the Christ they profess. To all who remain faithful to him, Jesus has said: "Him who overcomes I will make a pillar in the temple of my God. Never again will he leave it. *I will write on him the name of my God and the name of the city of my God*, the new Jerusalem, which is coming down out of heaven from my God" (Revelation 3:12).

Today take time to picture yourself in God's holy presence, with the name of his Son imprinted on your soul. Ask him for whatever you need, especially for the grace to realize that his eyes are always on you and his heart is always for you.

Wednesday

PRAYING THE NAME

You shall not take the name of the LORD your God in vain. (Exodus 20:7 NKJV)

Sing to the LORD, you saints of his,
praise his holy name. (Psalm 30:4)

Reflect On:	Psalm 30
Praise God:	Because he satisfies us with good things.
Offer Thanks:	For God's justice and compassion.
Confess:	Any tendency to speak or live in a way that dishonors God's name.
Ask God:	To help you live in a way that daily honors his name.

I've been called by various names in my life, but the one I liked least was "Sally." No doubt there are many wonderful Sallys in this world, but I am not and never will be one of them. So it irritated me whenever I ran into a woman I knew who could never seem to remember my name. As soon as we saw each other, Judy would break into a big smile and exclaim, "Sally, how are you?"—like she really meant it, like she really cared. Despite my initial irritation, Judy and I eventually became good friends—after she started calling me by my real name, of course.

Even though it's important to get someone's name right, names today have far less significance than they did in biblical times. In the Hebrew Scriptures names sometimes reflected the character or even the destiny of the person. Abigail's first husband, for instance, was a dim-witted man named Nabal, whose name means "fool."

Sarah, who laughed when an angel told her she would become pregnant at the age of ninety, gave birth to her son Isaac, which means "laughter." Abraham, who was a hundred years old when Isaac was born, means "the father of multitudes."

In God's case, there is an especially close relationship between his name and his nature. By revealing his name, God reveals who he is, allowing us access to him and placing himself within the reach of our prayers. Scripture tells us we can call on the name of the Lord and even take refuge in his name. By disclosing himself in this way, God not only makes himself accessible but vulnerable, allowing for the possibility that we will dishonor his name, using it as a common curse word or as a seal of divine approval on our own opinions or endeavors. We can also defile his name by claiming to belong to him though living in ways that contradict his character.

Today let us learn to cherish God's name, echoing the words of Jesus who taught his disciples to pray: "Our Father who art in heaven, hallowed be thy name."

Thursday

PRAYING THE NAME

Some trust in chariots and some in horses,
but we trust in the name of the LORD our God.
(Psalm 20:7)

Let him who walks in the dark,
who has no light,
trust in the name of the LORD
and rely on his God.
But now, all you who light fires
and provide yourselves with flaming torches,
go, walk in the light of your fires
and of the torches you have set ablaze.
This is what you shall receive from my hand:
You will lie down in torment. (Isaiah 50:10–11)

Reflect On: Isaiah 50:10–11
Praise God: For banishing our darkness through the light of Christ.
Offer Thanks: For God's readiness to help us in times of darkness.
Confess: Any tendency to seek safety apart from God.
Ask God: To help you see the futility of worrying rather than trusting.

One of my jobs as an eight-year-old was taking the garbage out right after dinner. It scared me silly because garbage disposal at our house involved dumping a portion of it into an old barrel, where it would later be burned (we hadn't heard of air pollution back then). It wouldn't have been so bad except that I had to walk at least a hundred yards in the dark before I could dump my smelly cargo and then run lickety-split back to safety. Realizing that an axe murderer or two was probably lurking at the edge of the woods bordering our home, I always took along a pearl-handled pistol, with a barrel at least twelve inches long. So what if it only shot caps? It comforted me and complemented my Hopalong Cassidy outfit rather nicely. I also hoped it would fool the resident maniacs and bad guys. It must have worked because I survived my eighth year without a single mishap!

When it comes to the dark, most children suffer as I did from an overactive imagination. But adults can have overactive imaginations too, even in daylight. We worry about whether our five-year-old will be ready for Harvard when the time comes, or whether a sudden frost will kill off the daffodils, or whether we'll be able to pour ourselves into last year's bathing suit. Such worries sound silly when you verbalize them. And though not all worries are so trivial, it remains true that worry is always counterproductive. It saps our energy and leads us down blind alleys as we conjure images of what *might* happen in the future. As a strategy for successful living, it's a complete failure.

God tells us that the antidote to worry is trust. He knows our limitations better than we do, realizing that when it comes to the future, we are all walking in the dark, unable to see past the minute we are living in. That's why he tells us to trust in his name, to count on his ability to see the future and prepare us for it—whatever may happen.

He also knows that trust and worry cannot coexist. We simply cannot *do* both at the same time. If we fail to trust him and instead rely on our own "light," our own limited understanding, we will find ourselves robbed of sleep and tormented by worry. Learning to trust in God's name in the darkest of times will enable us to lie down in peace, knowing we are safe.

Friday

PROMISES ASSOCIATED WITH GOD'S NAME

Mercy, protection, blessing—these are the concrete promises, the gifts that belong to everyone who loves God's name. If you love his name, God will always hear your prayers. He will sooner or later help you find a way out of trouble. He will grant mercy enough for your failings. Loving God's name means upholding his reputation by reflecting his character, by trusting him, and by praying in a way that acknowledges his nature—that he is full of power, love, goodness, and faithfulness. God's name holds so many blessings for the faithful that it's no wonder the psalmist exhorts us to rejoice in God's name all day long (see Psalm 89:16–17).

Promises in Scripture

"Because he loves me," says the LORD, "I will rescue him;
I will protect him, for he acknowledges my name.
He will call upon me, and I will answer him;
I will be with him in trouble,
I will deliver him and honor him." (Psalm 91:14–15)

Turn to me and have mercy on me,
as you always do to those who love your name. (Psalm 119:132)

The LORD will establish you as his holy people, as he promised you on oath, if you keep the commands of the LORD your God and walk in his ways. Then all the peoples on earth will see that you are called by the name of the LORD, and they will fear you. The LORD will grant you abundant prosperity—in the fruit of your womb, the young of your livestock and the crops of your ground—in the land he swore to your forefathers to give you. (Deuteronomy 28:9–11)

Continued Prayer and Praise

Pray that God will get the glory for every good thing you do. (Psalm 115:1)

Pray God's name when you wake in the middle of the night. (Psalm 119:55)

Call on the name of the Lord for help in the midst of difficulty. (Psalm 124:8)

17

KING

MELEK

The Name

The Israelites believed that *Yahweh* was *Melek,* or King—not just over Israel but over every nation on earth. They understood that the temple in Jerusalem was the earthly symbol of God's heavenly throne, and they expected a coming Messiah who would one day save his people from their enemies, establishing his rule over the whole world.

The New Testament presents Jesus as the King of kings, whose perfect obedience ushered in the kingdom of heaven. For the last two thousand years, God's kingdom has continued to spread through every nation, tribe, people, and language, as men and women accept Christ's rule. When you pray to *Yahweh Melek*, you are praying to the God who watches over the whole earth and who will one day come in glory to usher in an eternal kingdom of peace and righteousness.

Key Scripture

Endow the king with your justice, O God,
the royal son with your righteousness.
He will judge your people in righteousness,
your afflicted ones with justice.
The mountains will bring prosperity to the people,
the hills the fruit of righteousness. (Psalm 72:1–3)

Monday

God Reveals His Name

Endow the king with your justice, O God,
the royal son with your righteousness.
He will judge your people in righteousness,
your afflicted ones with justice.
The mountains will bring prosperity to the people,
the hills the fruit of righteousness.
He will defend the afflicted among the people
and save the children of the needy;
he will crush the oppressor.
He will endure as long as the sun,
as long as the moon, through all generations.
He will be like rain falling on a mown field,
like showers watering the earth.
In his days the righteous will flourish;
prosperity will abound till the moon is no more.
He will rule from sea to sea
and from the River to the ends of the earth. . . .
All kings will bow down to him
and all nations will serve him.
For he will deliver the needy who cry out,
the afflicted who have no one to help.
He will take pity on the weak and the needy
and save the needy from death.
He will rescue them from oppression and violence,
for precious is their blood in his sight.
Long may he live! (Psalm 72:1–8, 11–15)

Lord, my God and King, come and rule over us. Defend the afflicted. Look with mercy on the weak and the needy. Rescue us from oppression and violence and be our King forever.

Understanding the Name

Compared to surrounding nations, the Israelites were relatively late in adopting monarchy as a form of government. Instead, they thought of *Yahweh* as their King. Once the monarchy was established, it was understood that the king received his power from God and was therefore responsible for ruling according to God's laws. David, Israel's second king, represented the ideal of how a king should rule. But most of the kings of Israel and Judah fell far short of the ideal, leading people away from God by forging ill-fated alliances with foreign powers and by sanctioning the worship of false gods. After years of living under the rule of these less-than-perfect kings, God's people longed for a Messiah—a descendant of David who would sit on Israel's throne, subdue its enemies, and then rule over the entire earth. Given these expectations, it is hardly surprising that even Jesus' disciples thought he would establish an earthly kingdom.

Studying the Name

1. This psalm may have been a coronation prayer for one of the Davidic kings. Though it doesn't directly refer to God as the King, it does reflect the values of our heavenly King. Describe these.
2. How would the world be different if today's rulers reflected the values expressed in this psalm?
3. This psalm can also be read as a messianic psalm. How did Jesus fulfill this prayer?
4. How have you experienced Jesus' rule in your own life? What difference has it made?

Tuesday

Praying the Name

A shoot will come up from the stump of Jesse;
from his roots a Branch will bear fruit.
The Spirit of the Lord *will rest on him—*
the Spirit of wisdom and of understanding,
the Spirit of counsel and of power,
the Spirit of knowledge and of the fear of the Lord*. . . .*
Righteousness will be his belt
and faithfulness the sash around his waist.
The wolf will live with the lamb,
the leopard will lie down with the goat,
the calf and the lion and the yearling together;
and a little child will lead them. . . .
The infant will play near the hole of the cobra,
and the young child put his hand into the viper's nest.
They will neither harm nor destroy
on all my holy mountain,
for the earth will be full of the knowledge of the Lord
as the waters cover the sea. (Isaiah 11:1–3, 5–6, 8–9)

Reflect On: Isaiah 11:1–9
Praise God: For he is the true King.
Offer Thanks: For the ways God has already used you to build up his kingdom.
Confess: Any tendency to live as though this world is all there is.
Ask God: To fill the earth with the knowledge of him.

Several years ago I nearly met a king. I was touring Israel and Jordan with a small group of editors and writers interested in learning more about the intractable problems of the region. During our time in Amman, Jordan, our tour director attempted to arrange a meeting with His Majesty King Hussein bin Talal, known to his people as *Al-Malik Al-Insan*, "The Humane King." But the king was busy that day. So we met, instead, with his younger brother, His Royal Highness Prince El Hassan bin Talal, who was then the crown prince. Afterward, we crowded around on the steps of the palace to have our photograph taken with him, commemorating our one brief brush with royalty.

Like most Americans, I find the idea of royalty exotic, romantic, and rather antiquated. And no wonder. Monarchs and monarchies have suffered a long decline throughout the world. If you doubt it, try an Internet word search for "king." You are more likely to turn up "Burger King," "B. B. King," "Martin Luther King," "Stephen King," "the Lion King," or even "Elvis Presley" than the name of a reigning monarch.

But the Bible pictures God as the greatest Monarch of all. Far from being in decline, God's rule extends over the entire universe. Though challenged by the one Jesus called "the prince of this world," God still reigns.

Isaiah presents a shocking though beautiful image of what the world will be like when God's rule is perfectly and permanently established: "The infant will play near the hole of the cobra"; "the wolf will live with the lamb"; "the leopard will lie down with the goat"; and "a little child will lead them." The world in perfect harmony. No violence, no hatred, no hurt. Nothing out of sync, out of control, off kilter. The weak and the strong living happily together, world without end. Evil will vanish, becoming merely an archaic word in the celestial dictionary.

Next time you read the newspaper or watch the nightly news, contrast Isaiah's vision of the world as it will one day be with your vision of the world as it currently is. Pray for the grace to perceive more deeply and to participate more fully in the work God is doing to build up his kingdom right now. Remember the words of Jesus shortly before his death: "The man who loves his life will lose it, while the man who hates his life in this world will keep it for eternal life. Whoever serves me must follow me; and where I am, my servant also will be" (John 12:25–26). Then join your prayer to his: *Our Father in heaven, hallowed be your name, your kingdom come, your will be done on earth, as it is in heaven.* (Matthew 6:9–10)

Wednesday

PRAYING THE NAME

The LORD reigns, let the earth be glad;
let the distant shores rejoice.
Clouds and thick darkness surround him;
righteousness and justice are the foundation of his throne.
Fire goes before him
and consumes his foes on every side.
His lightning lights up the world;
the earth sees and trembles. (Psalm 97:1–4)

Reflect On: Psalm 97
Praise God: For his reign over the entire world.
Offer Thanks: That justice is foundational to God's kingdom.
Confess: Any sin you have been reluctant to admit.
Ask God: To extend his reign over you and through you.

Several years ago I was in Dallas enjoying dinner with friends in a restaurant located on the top floor of a downtown hotel. A summer thunderstorm provided the dramatic backdrop for our meal. Midway through, we were dazzled by a flash of lightning striking a nearby electrical grid and plunging a sector of the city into darkness. As Mark Twain once observed, "Thunder is good, thunder is impressive; but it is lightning that does the work."

In the middle of a violent storm, the old canard that thunder is merely the sound of angels bowling no longer provides comfort to my eight-year-old, who just last week was certain that lightning was about to strike our house, despite my reasoned assurances to the contrary. (The next day I discovered that lightning had indeed struck, not in our yard, but in the yard of friends who live nearby, felling a tree and burning a hole in the ground.)

Thunder and lightning are impressive phenomena no matter how old you are. I had a slightly nutty friend who used to run around like Henny Penny during thunderstorms, asking—half in jest—whether anyone had any "unrepented sin in their life."

The psalmist portrays God as the greatest of all kings, who rules over the entire created world. His decrees move not only nations and peoples but even mountains, which melt like wax before him. His lightning lights up the world. Remember this majestic portrait of our heavenly King the next time you are jarred from your sleep by a sudden storm. Before you nod off to sleep again, take a moment to ask him to cleanse your heart, to deal with the sins you haven't even admitted to yourself. Ask him to extend his kingdom by working in you and through you. Then praise him for his greatness, remembering that the psalmist says the foundations of his throne are righteousness and justice.

Thursday

PRAYING THE NAME

God is the King of all the earth. (Psalm 47:7)

Jesus told them another parable: "The kingdom of heaven is like a man who sowed good seed in his field. But while everyone was sleeping, his enemy came and sowed weeds among the wheat, and went away. When the wheat sprouted and formed heads, then the weeds also appeared.

"The owner's servants came to him and said, 'Sir, didn't you sow good seed in your field? Where then did the weeds come from?'

" 'An enemy did this,' he replied.

"The servants asked him, 'Do you want us to go and pull them up?'

" 'No,' he answered, 'because while you are pulling the weeds, you may root up the wheat with them. Let both grow together until the harvest. At that time I will tell the harvesters: First collect the weeds and tie them in bundles to be burned; then gather the wheat and bring it into my barn.' " (Matthew 13:24–30)

Reflect On: Psalm 47 and Matthew 13:24–30
Praise God: The King of the whole earth.
Offer Thanks: For God's patience.
Confess: Any complacency you may have regarding the return of the King.
Ask God: To hasten the coming of his Son.

If God is King of the whole world, why is the world such a mess? Couldn't an all-powerful God do something about the poverty, crime, and suffering that have been part of the world's story from the beginning? Wouldn't an all-loving God want to?

The question nags. It's hard to ignore. It demands our attention. Perhaps it will help if we consider two things: First, there's opposition. Satan (the word means "Adversary") is a spiritual being, a fallen angel, who opposed God's rule and in so doing ushered sin into the world. And sin is at the root of every misery the world has ever suffered.

Second, though God could have instantly destroyed Satan and sinners (that's all of us), he decided to take the long way round, quelling the world's rebellion not by brute force but by the power of divine love. That strategy requires restraint. It takes patience. It means justice in a final sense has to be delayed. It means evil is played out to the bitter end so that love can draw as many people as possible into the net of the kingdom. To say it another way, the weeds and the wheat are allowed to grow up together until the world's last day.

On that day Jesus will no longer hide himself but will step boldly into history, not veiling his power, but appearing in all his brilliance as King of kings and Lord of lords, judging the world with his justice and establishing his reign on the earth.

As we wait for the King's return, let's spread the kingdom by sharing the good news, feeding the hungry, serving the poor, and loosening the bonds of the oppressed. Also, let us allow the values of the kingdom to shine forth in us by the way we think and act and pray. Then, anticipating that final day of the Lord, let us bow down and worship, proclaiming Jesus as our King and Lord forever.

Friday

PROMISES ASSOCIATED WITH GOD'S NAME

Jesus promised his followers that they would inherit the kingdom of God, prepared for them since the beginning of time. Take a few moments to consider what your life would look like if you really believed that in just a few short years, you were going to inherit a kingdom, filled with everything your heart desired. This would be a place so marvelous that in it you would never be lonely, confused, or bored. A place so peaceful that you would always love and be loved, understand and be understood. Every need, every desire would be perfectly fulfilled.

Wouldn't this knowledge put things in an entirely different perspective? Would life be nearly as frantic? Would you expend so much energy stockpiling the goods of this world? Or would you find a new ease settling into your soul and a growing desire to get ready for the world to come by reflecting its values right here and right now?

Promises in Scripture

The LORD will be king over the whole earth. On that day there will be one LORD, and his name the only name. (Zechariah 14:9)

The righteous will shine like the sun in the kingdom of their Father. (Matthew 13:43)

Then the King will say to those on his right, "Come, you who are blessed by my Father; take your inheritance, the kingdom prepared for you since the creation of the world." (Matthew 25:34)

Then I saw a new heaven and a new earth, for the first heaven and the first earth had passed away, and there was no longer any sea. I saw the

Holy City, the new Jerusalem, coming down out of heaven from God, prepared as a bride beautifully dressed for her husband. And I heard a loud voice from the throne saying, "Now the dwelling of God is with men, and he will live with them. They will be his people, and God himself will be with them and be their God. He will wipe every tear from their eyes. There will be no more death or mourning or crying or pain, for the old order of things has passed away." (Revelation 21:1–4)

Continued Prayer and Praise

Pray for the increase of God's government. (Isaiah 9:6–7)

Worship the King of glory. (Psalm 24)

Approach the throne of grace with confidence. (Hebrews 4:16)

Envision the throne of God and of the Lamb. (Revelation 22:1–5)

18

Husband

Ish

The Name

Ish is the Hebrew word for "husband" in Hosea 2:16. The word *baal* in the Hebrew Scriptures can also be translated "husband" (as well as "lord," "owner," or "master"), though it usually refers to the Canaanite fertility god Baal (*baal* does occur in Hosea 2:16, "master"). Remarkably, in Isaiah and Jeremiah, this is also used to describe God as the husband of his people Israel. Though we never pray to *baal,* we do pray to the God who is the ideal husband, the one who provides for and protects his people and who refuses to divorce us no matter how unfaithful we may be. In the New Testament Jesus is presented as the bridegroom and the church as his bride.

Key Scripture

"In that day," declares the LORD,
    "you will call me 'my husband';
    you will no longer call me 'my master.' . . .
I will betroth you to me forever;
    I will betroth you in righteousness and justice,
    in love and compassion.
I will betroth you in faithfulness,
    and you will acknowledge the LORD." (Hosea 2:16, 19–20)

Monday

GOD REVEALS HIS NAME

When the LORD began to speak through Hosea, the LORD said to him, "Go, take to yourself an adulterous wife and children of unfaithfulness, because the land is guilty of the vilest adultery in departing from the LORD." So he married Gomer. . . .

She said, "I will go after my lovers,
who give me my food and my water,
my wool and my linen, my oil and my drink."
Therefore I will block her path with thornbushes;
I will wall her in so that she cannot find her way.
She will chase after her lovers but not catch them;
she will look for them but not find them.
Then she will say,
"I will go back to my husband as at first,
for then I was better off than now." . . .
"In that day," declares the LORD,
"you will call me 'my husband';
you will no longer call me 'my master.' . . .
I will betroth you to me forever;
I will betroth you in righteousness and justice,
in love and compassion.
I will betroth you in faithfulness,
and you will acknowledge the LORD. . . ."

The LORD said to me, "Go, show your love to your wife again, though she is loved by another and is an adulteress. Love her as the LORD loves the Israelites, though they turn to other gods." (From Hosea 1–3)

Lord and the lover of our souls, call to us again and revive our love for you. Receive us graciously and we will praise your forever, our faithful God. Amen.

Understanding the Name

God's passionate love for Israel is reflected in the Hebrew word *Ish* (EESH), meaning "husband." When it is applied to God in the Hebrew Scriptures, it symbolizes the ideal relationship between God and Israel. God is the perfect husband—loving, forgiving, and faithful, providing for and protecting his people. This metaphor of monogamous marriage between God and his people is strengthened in the New Testament, which reveals Jesus as the loving, sacrificial bridegroom of the church. Our destiny, our greatest purpose as God's people, is to become his bride.

Studying the Name

1. Put yourself in Hosea's place and imagine what you would feel like if your spouse were a prostitute or a womanizer. Now think about how God feels when his people stray from him. How do you think God responds to unfaithfulness?
2. What encouragement for your own life can you take from the story of Hosea and Gomer?
3. What encouragement can you take for the church?

Tuesday

PRAYING THE NAME

I will betroth you to me forever;
I will betroth you in righteousness and justice,
in love and compassion.
I will betroth you in faithfulness,
and you will acknowledge the LORD. *(Hosea 2:19–20)*

Reflect On: Hosea 1; 2:16–20
Praise God: Because he is not power or knowledge or wealth but he *is* love.
Offer Thanks: That God has pursued an intimate relationship with you.
Confess: Any tendency to settle for less in your relationship with God than he intends.
Ask God: To reveal himself to you as the one who loves you *no matter what.*

My maternal grandparents, Earl and Opal Dunbar, were the original odd couple, at least in certain superficial respects. She was a short woman, whose head didn't reach his shoulders, even on tiptoe. She had only an eighth-grade education, while he graduated from a private men's college. He was a chemist and an entrepreneur, and she was a housewife who cared for their two daughters. Despite their superficial differences they were devoted to each other.

When it comes to love and marriage, the strangest match in all of history is the one between God and his people. At first glance it looks like a complete mismatch! A holy God linked to weak and sinful human beings. Greatness linked to smallness. Wisdom linked to folly. Yet God says: "I will betroth you to me forever." This is his intent, his idea, his plan. Whether you are a man or a woman, married or single, makes no difference. Because you are a member of his people, God wants you to know him as your protector, as friend and provider, as the lover of your soul—as your husband.

Let's not settle, then, for a relationship that keeps God at arm's length, one that expects little from him and experiences less. Instead, we can allow him to close the gap between our smallness and his greatness, our sin and his holiness, our weakness and his power. We can lower our guard, being honest about our longings and our need for him. We can acknowledge that we want him more than anything or anyone. And we can plead with him to open our souls to his faithful, intimate love.

Take some time today to think about how an ideal husband provides for his wife. Now think about how the ideal wife responds. Ask God to give you the grace to respond in the same way—with faithfulness, trust, and gratitude, as well as the ever-increasing joy that belongs to all those who love God.

Wednesday

PRAYING THE NAME

The LORD said to me, "Go, show your love to your wife again, though she is loved by another and is an adulteress. Love her as the LORD loves the Israelites, though they turn to other gods." (Hosea 3:1)

Reflect On:	Hosea 1 and 3
Praise God:	Because his love does not blow hot and cold but is constant.
Offer Thanks:	For the times God has pursued you despite your own unfaithfulness or lack of interest.
Confess:	Any tendency to take your relationship with God for granted.
Ask God:	To give you a heart of obedience to express your love for him.

Most of us realize that our choice of a marriage partner is one of the most important decisions we will ever make. We may even expect God's help with such a critical decision. But few of us would expect or welcome the kind of help Hosea received when it came time for him to marry. A prophet in the northern kingdom of Israel, Hosea started his ministry by obeying these surprising instructions from the Lord regarding his future spouse: "Go, take to yourself an adulterous wife." What?! Why would God tell Hosea to marry a woman who would break his heart and make a fool of him?

To make a point. To paint a picture. To get his people's attention.

Hosea's life became a lived-out prophecy—a picture of God's own experience of faithless Israel. Hosea's wife proved wayward just as Israel had. She provoked him, just as Israel had provoked God. But, incredibly, instead of abandoning the wife who had abandoned him, Hosea ran after her, pursued her, and brought her home again. And that's the message! God running after his people, showing his love to us again and again, and calling us back to a faithful and fulfilling relationship.

Let Hosea's constant love for his wayward wife reveal God's unfailing love for you and for his people. Ask him to forgive your unfaithfulness and to increase your longing so that you can fully enter into the relationship he intends for you.

Thursday

PRAYING THE NAME

You shall not make for yourself an idol in the form of anything in heaven above or on the earth beneath or in the waters below. You shall not bow down to them or worship them; for I, the LORD your God, am a jealous God. (Exodus 20:4–5)

Reflect On:	Exodus 20:4–5
Praise God:	Because he alone can satisfy us.
Offer Thanks:	That God has not left you in the dark but has revealed himself to you.
Confess:	Any attachment to things or people that gets in the way of your relationship with God.
Ask God:	To free you so that you can worship him in spirit and in truth.

My daughter Katie was horrified when she first heard about idol worship. She was only six when she rushed into the house with the startling news: "Mom, do you know that some people worship cats!" She was incredulous, assuring me that she would never worship our cat. Of course I was relieved, aware as I am that she has Pipi on a pedestal, sure that she is the best cat in the world. Still, I couldn't help wonder what friends and family members might think had she started building little cat altars around the house, heaped with offerings of kitty litter and catnip, and saucers full of goldfish.

I'm not sure where Katie got her information about cat worship, but I am pretty sure she didn't have a clue about the variety of shapes, sizes, and colors that today's new and improved idols come in. Had she read the Scripture passage above, she might simply have considered idol worship an archaic problem with little relevance today.

But the truth is idolatry is still a big problem, even in America, even in the twenty-first century. Think about those svelte bodies that parade themselves in front of you on television or at the theater. Or the dream house beckoning from the magazine on your coffee table. Or the exotic vacation or the corner office or the fat paycheck or the perfect retirement home. Whatever it is—even good things, even blessings—can seduce us so that we end up spending ourselves on them rather than on God.

The poet William Cowper penned a verse in the eighteenth century that would make a fitting prayer for us today:

The dearest idol I have known,
Whate'er that idol be,
Help me to tear it from thy throne,
And worship only thee.

To gauge your own susceptibility to idols, take this week—all seven days of it—and scrutinize how you spend three precious resources: your time, your talents, and your money. If you are brave, you might even try drawing a pie chart to gauge what portion of each day's waking hours you spend thinking about God and the things he cares about. If you find that you're spending precious little on God and that you've formed any idolatrous attachments, take time to seek him, begging his forgiveness and asking him to free you. As you rededicate your life to God, remember that you will be calling down his blessing, not just on yourself and your children, but on a thousand generations yet to come.

Friday

PROMISES ASSOCIATED WITH GOD'S NAME

"For better or for worse, for richer or poorer, in sickness and in health, 'til death us do part." This traditional wedding vow sounds impressive, solid, unbreakable. Yet it is still only a temporary promise, one that dissolves the moment a spouse dies. In truth only God has the power to promise us undying love. Remember this the next time you are tempted to think he has abandoned you, the next time you are on the verge of believing he's turned his back on you. Remember, too, the words of Paul, who assures us that nothing in all creation (and *nothing* means *nothing*) "will be able to separate us from the love of God that is in Christ Jesus our Lord" (Romans 8:39).

Promises in Scripture

"For your Maker is your husband—
the LORD Almighty is his name—
the Holy One of Israel is your Redeemer;
he is called the God of all the earth.
The LORD will call you back
as if you were a wife deserted and distressed in spirit—
a wife who married young,
only to be rejected," says your God.
"For a brief moment I abandoned you,
but with deep compassion I will bring you back.
In a surge of anger
I hid my face from you for a moment
but with everlasting kindness
I will have compassion on you,"
says the LORD your Redeemer. (Isaiah 54:5–8)

No longer will they call you Deserted,
or name your land Desolate.

But you will be called Hephzibah [meaning "my delight is in her"],
and your land Beulah [meaning "married"];
for the LORD will take delight in you
and your land will be married.
As a young man marries a maiden
so will your sons marry you;
as a bridegroom rejoices over his bride,
so will your God rejoice over you. (Isaiah 62:4–5)

Continued Prayer and Praise

Pray for yourself and for the church to remain faithful to God. (Jeremiah 3:14, 20)

Remember that God is jealous for you. (Exodus 5:8–10 and 34:14)

Be glad of God's fierce love for you. (Song of Songs 8:6–7)

Reflect on Christ's love for you as a member of his church. (Ephesians 5:25–30)

19

Living God

El Chay

The Name

This title sets Israel's God apart from the false gods of the surrounding nations. Unlike idols of wood and stone, made by human hands, the Living God is himself Maker of heaven and earth. He alone is the source of our life. We live because he lives. The prophet Jeremiah reminded God's people that "every goldsmith is shamed by his idols. His images are a fraud; they have no breath in them" (Jeremiah 10:14).

Key Scripture

And Hezekiah prayed to the LORD: "O LORD, God of Israel, enthroned between the cherubim, you alone are God over all the kingdoms of the earth. You have made heaven and earth. Give ear, O LORD, and hear; open your eyes, O LORD, and see; listen to the words Sennacherib has sent to insult the living God." (2 Kings 19:15–16)

Monday

God Reveals His Name

Now Sennacherib received a report that Tirhakah, the Cushite king of Egypt, was marching out to fight against him. So he again sent messengers to Hezekiah with this word: "Say to Hezekiah king of Judah: Do not let the god you depend on deceive you when he says, 'Jerusalem will not be handed over to the king of Assyria.' Surely you have heard what the kings of Assyria have done to all the countries, destroying them completely. And will you be delivered? Did the gods of the nations that were destroyed by my forefathers deliver them: the gods of Gozan, Haran, Rezeph and the people of Eden who were in Tel Assar? Where is the king of Hamath, the king of Arpad, the king of the city of Sepharvaim, or of Hena or Ivvah?"

Hezekiah received the letter from the messengers and read it. Then he went up to the temple of the LORD and spread it out before the LORD. And Hezekiah prayed to the LORD: "O LORD, God of Israel, enthroned between the cherubim, you alone are God over all the kingdoms of the earth. You have made heaven and earth. Give ear, O LORD, and hear; open your eyes, O LORD, and see; listen to the words Sennacherib has sent to insult the living God.

"It is true, O LORD, that the Assyrian kings have laid waste these nations and their lands. They have thrown their gods into the fire and destroyed them, for they were not gods but only wood and stone, fashioned by men's hands. Now, O LORD our God, deliver us from his hand, so that all kingdoms on earth may know that you alone, O LORD, are God."...

That night the angel of the LORD went out and put to death a hundred and eighty-five thousand men in the Assyrian camp. When the people got up the next morning—there were all the dead bodies! So Sennacherib king of Assyria broke camp and withdrew. He returned to Nineveh and stayed there.

One day, while he was worshiping in the temple of his god Nisroch, his sons Adrammelech and Sharezer cut him down with the sword, and they escaped to the land of Ararat. And Esarhaddon his son succeeded him as king. (2 Kings 19:9–19, 35–37)

Lord, you are a God who speaks, who hears, and who acts. Thank you for making me and breathing life into me. Please watch over me and hear me when I cry out to you; deliver me from my enemies and glorify your name so that everyone who knows me may know that you alone are El Chay, the Living God. Amen.

Understanding the Name

Scripture constantly warns against the worship of false gods. The first of the Ten Commandments is itself a proscription against idol worship. The title *El Chay* (EL CHAY), the Living God, emphasizes God's role as Creator of all that is, in contrast with idols made of metal, wood, or stone, which are merely the creations of human hands. Jeremiah paints a vivid picture, saying, "The customs of the peoples are worthless; they cut a tree out of the forest, and a craftsman shapes it with his chisel. They adorn it with silver and gold; they fasten it with hammer and nails so it will not totter. Like a scarecrow in a melon patch, their idols cannot speak; they must be carried because they cannot walk. Do not fear them; they can do no harm nor can they do any good" (Jeremiah 10:3–5). Imagine praying to a deaf and dumb god! That's exactly the case when someone worships any other God than *El Chay*!

Studying the Name

1. Sennacherib ruled Assyria and Babylonia from 705–681 B.C. He invaded Judah in 701 B.C. and threatened to attack Jerusalem when King Hezekiah refused to pay taxes. How does Hezekiah's prayer reflect his understanding of the "Living God"?

2. Though Hezekiah asked God to deliver his people from their enemies, his prayer primarily focused on God's honor. How can his prayer be a model for ours?
3. How can this story of Hezekiah's reliance on the Living God to defend his people be applied in the lives of God's people today? In your own life?

Tuesday

Praying the Name

O Lord, God of Israel, enthroned between the cherubim, you alone are God over all the kingdoms of the earth. You have made heaven and earth. Give ear, O Lord, and hear; open your eyes, O Lord, and see; listen to the words Sennacherib has sent to insult the living God.

It is true, O Lord, that the Assyrian kings have laid waste these nations and their lands. They have thrown their gods into the fire and destroyed them, for they were not gods but only wood and stone, fashioned by men's hands. Now, O Lord our God, deliver us from his hand, so that all kingdoms on earth may know that you alone, O Lord, are God. (2 Kings 19:15–19)

Reflect On:	2 Kings 19:14–37
Praise God:	Because he is God over all the earth.
Offer Thanks:	Because God hears your prayers and sees your need.
Confess:	Any lack of prayerfulness for yourself, your family, your community, or the world.
Ask God:	To deliver you from your enemies.

Hezekiah looked out over the siege works surrounding Jerusalem, reviewing his preparations for the inevitable assault. He had rebuilt the city's walls, constructed strong towers, and produced a large cache of weapons and shields with which to repel the Assyrian invasion. The tunnel beneath Jerusalem had been his greatest achievement, ensuring the city's water supply. But even it could not guarantee Jerusalem's safety. For Sennacherib had already crushed forty-six towns in Judah and carried off tens of thousands of captives. He had also invaded a city twenty miles to the west, taking its elders and flaying them alive as punishment for the city's disloyalty.

Hezekiah held a letter in his hand. Now he raised it to the light and read the words of Sennacherib: "Do not let the god you depend on deceive you when he says, 'Jerusalem will not be handed over to the king of Assyria.'"

Clutching the letter to his breast, King Hezekiah hurried to the temple, prostrating himself before the Lord and spreading it out as evidence against his enemy. "Give ear, O Lord, and hear; open your eyes, O Lord, and see; listen to the words Sennacherib has sent to insult the living God."

Unlike gods of wood and stone, fashioned by the hands of living men, Hezekiah knew that it was the Living God himself—the One who had fashioned both heaven and earth—who would determine the fate of nations. So the king of Judah prayed and trusted. Then with his own eyes he saw the deliverance God devised for his people, destroying an enemy that had seemed invincible in the course of a single night.

But what has his story to do with ours? Like it or not, we all have enemies with which to contend, though often these enemies come from inside rather than outside. We have trouble controlling our anger. We become addicted to something or someone. We fall into depression. Things look hopeless. Each of us can name our poison—the problem that looms so large we think it is beyond God's power to deliver us.

Whatever difficulties besiege you today, reject the lie that they cannot be defeated and then lay out your complaint to the Lord, praying:

Listen, O Lord, and hear; open your eyes, O Lord, and see. Though my enemy is strong, you are stronger still. Deliver me from evil and today bring glory to your name. For you are the Living God who loves me—the One who sees, who hears, and who always acts to save me. Amen.

Wednesday

PRAYING THE NAME

For who is there of all flesh that has heard the voice of the living God speaking out of fire, as we have. . . ? (Deuteronomy 5:26 NRSV*)*

Joshua said to the Israelites, "Come here and listen to the words of the LORD *your God. This is how you will know that the living God is among you and that he will certainly drive out before you the Canaanites, Hittites, Hivites, Perizzites, Girgashites, Amorites and Jebusites." (Joshua 3:9–10)*

Reflect On:	Joshua 3:9–10
Praise God:	For his saving actions.
Offer Thanks:	For the ways God has driven out your enemies.
Confess:	Any tendency to believe that God is unable or unwilling to act on your behalf.
Ask God:	To drive out the enemies that continue to harass you.

There was a time in my life when I doubted God's existence. For a brief time, I even considered myself an atheist. But I hadn't the stamina for it, so I settled instead into a long and comfortable agnosticism. Maybe God existed, maybe he didn't. I neither knew nor cared. I was nineteen years old and living on a college campus with 40,000 other students, many of whom had embraced the anything-goes mantra of the late 1960s and early 1970s. We all chanted it together: "What's true for you is true for you, and what's true for me is true for me."

For the next few years I lived without much of a moral compass. Then, after graduating, I found myself in a dead-end job in the middle of nowhere working for next to nothing. Away from friends, away from drugs and the freewheeling way of life I had developed on campus, I had to grapple with life and figure out where mine was heading. Nowhere, was the frightening conclusion. As the months wore on, I began to feel hopeless, not just about my career prospects, but about life in general. If truth was relative, as I had concluded, then life had no meaning—my life had no meaning. I felt a growing sense of isolation and frustration.

It was into this emptiness that thoughts about God crept in. A close friend spoke about faith in a way that utterly confounded me. Someone suggested I read C. S. Lewis's *Mere Christianity.* Gradually, my defenses thinned until I finally prayed my first real prayer, "God, I don't even know if you exist, but if you do, I need to know. Please reveal yourself to me." It wasn't eloquent. It wasn't faith-filled. But it was real.

After that, I asked "the God I wasn't even sure existed" to help me stop smoking. I had tried numerous times without the slightest success. For some reason my failed attempts at breaking this habit had come to symbolize my failures in the rest of life. So everyday I prayed, and everyday I had the strength not to pick up that first cigarette. Pretty soon I wasn't even thinking about smoking.

That early success gave way to more prayers and more success. I felt myself growing stronger and freer with the unshakable sense that there was a God who loved me. A powerful God was willing to exchange my weakness for his strength. It was like opening a Pandora's box of blessings. Once I lifted the lid, instead of troubles swarming out, so many good things happened that I began to believe there was nothing God and I couldn't do together.

Because of that early experience with God, I understand what Joshua meant when he told the Israelites, poised on the threshold of the Promised Land: "This is how you will know that the living God is among you and that he will certainly drive out before you the Canaanites, Hittites, Hivites, Perizzites, Girgashites, Amorites and Jebusites." I knew God was with me because he was driving out my enemies—my addiction, my fear, the sense of hopelessness and meaninglessness—and replacing them with his blessings—with freedom, confidence, peace, and a sense of purpose.

Today, you may be facing enemies of your own. Pray to the Lord, asking him to drive them out before you, for that is how you will know that *El Chay,* the Living God, is alive and well, working out his good plan for your life. He is a God who hears, who speaks, and who stands ready to work his wonders in your life.

Thursday

Praying the Name

You, however, are controlled not by the sinful nature but by the Spirit, if the Spirit of God lives in you. And if anyone does not have the Spirit of Christ, he does not belong to Christ. But if Christ is in you, your body is dead because of sin, yet your spirit is alive because of righteousness. And if the Spirit of him who raised Jesus from the dead is living in you, he who raised Christ from the dead will also give life to your mortal bodies through his Spirit, who lives in you. (Romans 8:9–11)

You yourselves are our letter, written on our hearts, known and read by everybody. You show that you are a letter from Christ, the result of our ministry, written not with ink but with the Spirit of the living God, not on tablets of stone but on tablets of human hearts. (2 Corinthians 3:2–3)

Reflect On: Romans 8:9–11; 2 Corinthians 3:2–3
Praise God: For his Word, which is living and active, sharper than a two-edged sword.
Offer Thanks: That the same Spirit who raised Jesus from the dead lives in you.
Confess: Any ambivalence you have toward yielding to God's Spirit.
Ask God: To help you taste the joys of the Spirit-controlled life.

Important as laws are, we know that the vitality of our faith cannot be measured solely in terms of life's "Thou Shalt Nots." To focus merely on outward conformity to a set of rules is to miss the point of the gospel: that God became human to share his essential life with us—to make us not just his servants but his dwelling place.

Incredibly, Scripture assures us that the Spirit of the Living God indwells all those who believe in his Son, Jesus.

But why, you may wonder, do you sometimes find so little evidence of God's presence when you search your heart to find him? There may be several reasons, but I want to consider the main one that operates in my own life, preventing me from experiencing the full freedom and power of the Living God. I call it spiritual ambivalence. It's a condition in which one foot is planted in God's kingdom while the other is still planted in the world. It's a setup for failure, like trying to board a boat while keeping one foot on the dock or trying to ski downhill without forsaking the hilltop. You want the gospel to fit your life rather than fitting your life to the gospel.

Today, if you find that you suffer from even the slightest bit of spiritual ambivalence, join me in forsaking it. Face yourself squarely and without excuses. Tell the Lord you can no longer live without his ongoing daily guidance. Assure him that you no longer want to control your life but that you want to be controlled by his living, powerful Holy Spirit. Then underline your prayer by giving up a meal or by fasting for twenty-four hours as a way of humbling yourself in the presence of the Living God.

Friday

Promises Associated with God's Name

It is impossible to live at the beginning of the twenty-first century without being acutely aware of the problems of the Middle East. We know of its religious and political conflicts. But few of us realize that many of its tensions are rooted in the intractable problem of water. Former UN Secretary General Boutros Boutros-Ghali's assessment has been widely quoted: "The next war in the Near East will not be about politics but over water." In any region and in any age, water is a symbol of life. And no wonder—most people can survive for weeks without food but only three to four days without water.

Jesus spoke of the "living water" that is never in short supply for those who believe in him. Indeed, he promises a "spring of water welling up to eternal life" (John 4:14). This is the living water that comes from the Spirit of the Living, All-powerful God, who makes his home in us.

Promises in Scripture

The Samaritan woman said to him, "You are a Jew and I am a Samaritan woman. How can you ask me for a drink?" (For Jews do not associate with Samaritans.)

Jesus answered her, "If you knew the gift of God and who it is that asks you for a drink, you would have asked him and he would have given you living water."

"Sir," the woman said, "you have nothing to draw with and the well is deep. Where can you get this living water? Are you greater than our father Jacob, who gave us the well and drank from it himself, as did also his sons and his flocks and herds?"

Jesus answered, "Everyone who drinks this water will be thirsty again, but whoever drinks the water I give him will never thirst. Indeed, the water

I give him will become in him a spring of water welling up to eternal life." (John 4:9–13)

On the last and greatest day of the Feast, Jesus stood and said in a loud voice, "If anyone is thirsty, let him come to me and drink. Whoever believes in me, as the Scripture has said, streams of living water will flow from within him." By this he meant the Spirit, whom those who believed in him were later to receive. Up to that time the Spirit had not been given, since Jesus had not yet been glorified. (John 7:37–39)

Continued Prayer and Praise

Express your thirst for the Living God. (Psalm 42)

Affirm the folly of trusting in anything other than the Living God. (Jeremiah 10:7–16)

Praise the Living God for his saving power. (Daniel 6:16–27)

Acknowledge Jesus as the Son of the Living God. (Matthew 16:13–16)

Remember that we are the temple of the Living God. (2 Corinthians 6:16)

Worship the Living God. (Hebrew 12:18–24)

20

Dwelling Place, Refuge, Shield, Fortress, Strong Tower

Maon, Machseh, Magen, Metsuda, Migdal-Oz

The Names

These descriptive names for God often appear in clusters in the psalms as well as in other portions of the Scripture. When you pray to God your Refuge, Shield, Fortress, Dwelling Place, and Strong Tower, you are invoking the God who has promised to watch over you and keep you safe.

Key Scripture

He who dwells in the shelter of the Most High
will rest in the shadow of the Almighty.
I will say of the LORD, "He is my refuge and my fortress,
my God in whom I trust." (Psalm 91:1–2)

Monday

GOD REVEALS HIS NAME

He who dwells in the shelter of the Most High
will rest in the shadow of the Almighty.
I will say of the LORD, "He is my refuge and my fortress,
my God, in whom I trust."
Surely he will save you from the fowler's snare
and from the deadly pestilence.
He will cover you with his feathers,
and under his wings you will find refuge;
his faithfulness will be your shield and rampart.
You will not fear the terror of night,
nor the arrow that flies by day,
nor the pestilence that stalks in the darkness,
nor the plague that destroys at midday.
A thousand may fall at your side,
ten thousand at your right hand,
but it will not come near you.
You will only observe with your eyes
and see the punishment of the wicked.
If you make the Most High your dwelling—
even the LORD, who is my refuge—
then no harm will befall you,
no disaster will come near your tent.
For he will command his angels concerning you
to guard you in all your ways;
they will lift you up in their hands,
so that you will not strike your foot against a stone.
You will tread upon the lion and the cobra;
you will trample the great lion and the serpent.

"Because he loves me," says the Lord, "I will rescue
him;
I will protect him, for he acknowledges my name.
He will call upon me, and I will answer him;
I will be with him in trouble,
I will deliver him and honor him.
With long life will I satisfy him
and show him my salvation. (Psalm 91:1–16)

Lord, teach me to dwell in your shelter and to rest in your shadow. Be with me in trouble and watch over me in danger. Satisfy me with a long life, and I will sing your praises, my refuge and my fortress, my God, in whom I trust. Amen.

Understanding the Names

The Hebrew Scriptures reveal a God who dwells with his people—first in a tent in the wilderness and then in the Jerusalem temple. The New Testament takes this idea of God's dwelling place on earth a giant step further by revealing a God who wants to dwell not merely *with* his people but *within* his people. Occasionally, Scripture reverses this imagery in a wonderful way by picturing God himself as our Dwelling Place or *Maon* (ma-OHN).

Closely allied to this image of Dwelling Place is the idea of God as our Refuge or *Machseh* (mach-SEH). He is pictured as one to whom we can run for safety and security. The word "refuge" also appears in the Hebrew Scriptures in connection to Israel's "cities of refuge" (the Hebrew word in this instance is *miqlat*), where people could flee for safety if they had accidentally killed someone. These cities were strategically located so that anyone in Israel was within a day's journey of one.

A shield or *Magen* (ma-GAIN) is another image of God's protecting care. Ancient shields were often made of layered cowhide and were used in situations of close combat as well as to protect soldiers from rocks hurled from city walls.

In biblical times, some cities were enclosed by walls, 25 feet high and 15 to 25 feet thick. Farmers worked in the fields by day and then retreated within the city walls at night for protection. Large fortified cities also contained strongholds or strong towers that provided additional defense should the city's outer walls be breached. Like the other terms already mentioned, God is compared to a fortress or *Metsuda* (me-tsu-DAH) and to a strong tower or *Migdal-Oz* (mig-dal OHZ).

Studying the Name

1. One of the more unusual metaphors for God in the Bible is that of an eagle or a great bird under whose wings the righteous can shelter. Compare this with Jesus' more domestic image of a mother hen who longs to gather her chicks under her wings (see Matthew 23:37). How would your life be different if you were able to take shelter under "the wings of God"?
2. What is one of the characteristics of the person who experiences God as his or her refuge?
3. What do you think it means to rest in God? How have you experienced this rest?
4. What dangers does the psalmist list in Psalm 91? What promises from God does he cite?
5. What are the things you fear most?
6. What is the link between loving God and experiencing God's faithfulness?

Tuesday

PRAYING THE NAME

The LORD is a refuge for the oppressed,
a stronghold in times of trouble.
Those who know your name will trust in you,
for you, LORD, have never forsaken those who seek you. (Psalm 9:9–10)

Even though I walk
through the valley of the shadow of death,
I will fear no evil,
for you are with me;
your rod and your staff,
they comfort me.
You prepare a table before me
in the presence of my enemies.
You anoint my head with oil;
my cup overflows.
Surely goodness and love will follow me
all the days of my life,
and I will dwell in the house of the LORD
forever. (Psalm 23:4–6)

Reflect On: Psalm 9:9–10; Psalm 23
Praise God: Because he cares for the oppressed.
Offer Thanks: For the times God has been your refuge.
Confess: Times when you've taken refuge in anything and everything but God.
Ask God: To be a refuge for the oppressed of the world.

A few years ago, a young Liberian man experienced the truth of God's promise to be a refuge for the oppressed. His story takes place in the late 1990s, in the middle of Liberia's bloody civil war.

Joedafi was doing his best to stay alive while making the forty-five-mile trek on foot to the capital city of Monrovia, hoping for a chance to escape the fighting that raged around him. After he and his friends spotted several bodies rotting in the bush, he began crying out to God with the words of Psalm 23—"Even though I walk through the valley of the shadow of death. . . ."

Suddenly he and his companions were surrounded by soldiers. They had unwittingly wandered into Charles Taylor's rebel camp. When one of Joedafi's friends tried to resist, the rebels didn't hesitate—they slit his throat with a machete.

Joedafi was thrown into a crudely constructed jail, around which were strewn human bones and skulls. Knowing he would die if he didn't escape, he kept on praying Psalm 23. Then, after a few days, he was moved to a place deep within the forest. He reports what happened next:

> I began to feel that I would be set free by the Almighty God. I'm not sure how I came to have such a feeling, but it was ever there. This thought was quite wild, because I witnessed the soldiers' disregard for life. They made us drink from human skulls, bury dead bodies, and live on leaves.
>
> Yet Psalm 23 was giving me the feeling that out of this valley of the shadow of death, God would deliver me. In the past, I read my Bible daily and went to church. Now I believed that God would do something and prove himself. I had believed in the Lord and trusted him to lead me in my life. I took faith in the teaching I heard that the Lord delivers those who trust him and commit their ways to him.
>
> One evening, as I was dozing off to sleep, I heard a silent voice call my name, commanding me to rise up and walk away from my captors. It was so commanding, I obeyed

> instantly and walked past sleeping guards out onto the main road. I walked on spellbound and passed by many rebel soldiers along the road, but not one of them dared ask me any question. I walked through many check-points and wasn't stopped once.

Joedafi kept on walking, hour after hour, until he met someone willing to give him a ride to Monrovia, where he then boarded a ship for Ghana.

What a remarkable story of a man who trusted God to be his refuge and was not disappointed! Most of us will never face the kind of terror Joedafi describes, but we will pass through storms that test our faith. When that happens, remember that the same God who so miraculously rescued this man is your God too. Let him be the refuge you seek, your stronghold in time of trouble.

Today as you think about God's desire to be a refuge for his people, pray for believers throughout the world who are suffering the ravaging effects of poverty, war, famine, and natural disasters. Ask God to shelter and to save them. Find a way to help by giving generously of your time and resources so that others will experience the power of God's promises.

Wednesday

Praying the Name

But I will sing of your strength,
in the morning I will sing of your love;
for you are my fortress,
my refuge in times of trouble.
O my Strength, I sing praise to you;
you, O God, are my fortress, my loving God.
(Psalm 59:16–17)

Hear my cry, O God;
listen to my prayer.
From the ends of the earth I call to you,
I call as my heart grows faint;
lead me to the rock that is higher than I.
For you have been my refuge,
a strong tower against the foe. (Psalm 61:1–3)

Reflect On: Psalm 59:16–17 and Psalm 61:1–3
Praise God: Because he is a strong tower against all foes.
Offer Thanks: For his sustaining grace.
Confess: Any tendency to make God your *last* instead of your *first* resort when trouble heads your way.
Ask God: To open your eyes to his protective care, past and present.

Whenever my youngest has a nightmare, she clambers into my bed and then promptly falls asleep, leaving me clutching for covers and bracing myself while her pint-size body sprawls sideways, pushing me firmly to the bed's edge. If I complain, she trains her deep, brown eyes on mine and holds up little hands shaped like claws, as though to illustrate the monsters of her dreams. Then she exclaims, "But, Mom, I scared!"

I can remember crawling into bed as a child, imagining myself covered by an impregnable bubble, designed to keep me safe through the night. Except for the time my eldest brother, hiding beneath my bed, shot his hand out and grabbed my ankle as I climbed into bed, my imaginary bubble worked like a charm.

The truth is, even grown-ups have fears, and often for good reason. Take David, for instance. The Bible presents Psalm 59 as the young man's cry for help when Saul was watching his house, waiting for a chance to kill him. No wonder David called God his "fortress," his "refuge in time of trouble." How else could he defend himself against the overwhelming power of a king intent on murder?

But David's God was no make-believe bubble, protecting him from imaginary fears. He was a fortress, or in modern terms, he was like a missile defense system that could not be breached. He deflected every weapon forged against David until Saul was finally defeated and David sat on Israel's throne. As Psalm 46:1 puts it, David found that God was "an ever-present help in trouble."

Where do you find help when you are in trouble? How do you calm yourself when you are afraid? Do you bluff your way through? Do you run, hide, ignore, counterattack? Whatever your chosen style of dealing with fear, it will prove a flimsy defense if you do not learn that God wants to be your fortress, your first line of defense. Today, take some time to gather up your fears small and large, heaping them before the Lord in prayer. Here's a short list to get you started:

- failure
- rejection
- financial loss
- flying

- public speaking
- for your children
- for your marriage
- social fears
- illness
- accidents
- aging
- death

Whatever your list, ask God to deliver you from them. Make it your steady habit to run to him as your fortress. Do this by memorizing Scriptures about his power, love, and faithfulness. Thank him for his past protection. Call to mind his promises in the Bible. Make this verse, taken from the ancient Irish hymn "Be Thou My Vision," your regular prayer:

Be thou my breastplate, my sword for the fight,
Be thou my armor, and be thou my might,
Thou my soul's shelter, and thou my high tower,
Raise thou me heavenward, O Power of my power.

As you do these things, you will learn to rest in the powerful, encircling arms of the God who is far stronger than any method of self-defense you could ever devise.

Thursday

PRAYING THE NAME

Many are saying of me,
"God will not deliver him."
But you are a shield around me, O LORD;
you bestow glory on me and lift up my head.
(Psalm 3:2–3)

For our struggle is not against flesh and blood, but against the rulers, against the authorities, against the powers of this dark world and against the spiritual forces of evil in the heavenly realms. Therefore put on the full armor of God, so that when the day of evil comes, you may be able to stand your ground. . . . In addition to all this, take up the shield of faith, with which you can extinguish all the flaming arrows of the evil one. (Ephesians 6:12–13, 16)

Reflect On: Psalm 3:2–3; Ephesians 6:12–18
Praise God: For he is our shield.
Offer Thanks: For the ways God is building up your faith.
Confess: Any tendency to let your guard down by failing to exercise your faith.
Ask God: To make you aware of the spiritual battle.

They say the devil is in the details, and I think that's true, especially when it comes to the details of our most important relationships. It reminds me of a joke about a couple who claimed to have the perfect marriage. When asked what made their relationship so successful, the husband replied, "Oh, that's easy. We never argue because she makes all the small decisions and I make all the big ones.

She decides where we're going to live, where we're going to work, where our kids will go to school, and how we're going to spend our money. And I decide what to do about the big things, like nuclear proliferation, air pollution, and global warming."

The truth is, most of our important battles will not be fought on the world's stage but right here at home in the midst of our day-to-day lives. These battles often involve a spiritual dimension we can't afford to ignore.

My friend Sarah's son suffers from a neurological disorder that sometimes creates enormous havoc in their home. He flies into frequent rages, becomes hysterical over the slightest injury, and displays various kinds of obsessive-compulsive behaviors. Helping him when he's upset, my friend confided, is like trying to calm a tornado or lasso a hurricane.

Last week, while her husband was away on a business trip, their little boy had another meltdown, one so violent that it threw Sarah completely off. Her son made such terrible threats that Sarah decided to put the kitchen knives well out of reach. When the tantrum was finally over, my friend went upstairs to her bedroom, shut the door, and screamed at the top of her lungs. She couldn't take it anymore. Where was God in all this? Why wouldn't he heal her son? Didn't he care? She shouted at him. She cried. She slammed the door. She pounded her fist on the bed.

In the next few days help came, in the shape of a caring friend who spent time with her son, in the shape of a counselor who offered helpful advice, and in the shape of a word from Scripture that convinced my friend that God had not abandoned her or her child—indeed, he knew better than she what they were facing. She reminded herself that there was a spiritual component to the fight she was waging. When her son acted out, she was tempted to forget everything she knew about God—about his faithfulness, his love, and his desire to help. But that forgetfulness always threw her into despair about the future.

As Sarah has reflected on her life, she has come to realize that she is living a story. Like any story, it has tension, high points, and low points. There's wonder and joy and delight as well as pain and sorrow and suffering. She knows that God has entrusted her son to her for a reason. She can't see the story's end, though she's aware of the possibilities for good and for ill. But she is also aware of God's faithfulness. Moreover, she is convinced that faith, which is a shield against the lies of the evil one, is what will help her play the role she is supposed to in the story God is writing.

Your own story may hold its share of challenges to your faith. When you feel yourself slipping into discouragement, take hold of the words of Psalm 3: "You are a shield around me, O LORD; you bestow glory on me and lift up my head."

Friday

Promises Associated with God's Name

Over and over the promise is made—not just that God will *provide* a refuge but that he will *be* a refuge. But that promise cannot be fulfilled if we haven't enough sense to run to God whenever we are in trouble. What does it mean to "run to God"? Is it more than a pretty metaphor? Doesn't this "running," which the psalmist speaks of, involve praying as a first resort, aligning our lives with God's values, yielding to his Spirit, and trusting him to act for our good even when life seems the exact opposite of good?

Take a few moments to reflect on the trouble spots in your own life. What has kept you from experiencing God as your refuge? Have you been seeking shelter elsewhere? Are you angry at God for letting you down? Or have you dug yourself into a hole that you now think you have to dig yourself out of? Do you feel guilty and unworthy of God's help? Do you think your situation is impossible? Or are you merely the self-reliant type? Tell God today that you want to grasp, not just the theory of his faithfulness, but the experience of it. Run to him and you will.

Promises in Scripture

For surely, O Lord, you bless the righteous;
you surround them with your favor as with a shield. (Psalm 5:12)

When calamity comes, the wicked are brought down,
but even in death the righteous have a refuge. (Proverbs 14:32)

The name of the Lord is a strong tower;
the righteous run to it and are safe. (Proverbs 18:10)

Continued Prayer and Praise

Dwelling Place

Express your longing to dwell with God. (Psalm 27:4–5)

Pray for those who are falsely accused. (Psalm 31:20)

Envision God as your dwelling place. (Psalm 90:1–2)

Recall how lovely is God's dwelling place. (Psalm 84)

Refuge

Remember that God cares for those who trust him. (Nahum 1:7)

Believe that the Lord is an ever-present help. (Psalm 46:1)

Know that the eternal God is our refuge. (Deuteronomy 33:27)

Find rest in God. (Psalm 62:5–7)

Shield

Be confident because God is your shield and great reward. (Genesis 15:1)

Remember that God is a shield and helper against enemies. (Deuteronomy 33:29)

Call on the Lord, who is your strength and your shield. (Psalm 28:7)

Rejoice because the Lord God is a sun and shield. (Psalm 84:11)

Fortress

Proclaim that the Lord is your fortress and deliverer. (2 Samuel 22:1–3)

Refuse to give in to fear because God is your fortress. (Psalm 46:2–7)

Let your soul find rest in God. (Psalm 62:1–2)

Strong Tower

Remember that God is a strong tower against the foe. (Psalm 61:3)

21

Judge

שֹׁפֵט

Shophet

The Name

Justice is ultimately rooted not in a collection of laws or rules but in the very character and nature of God. As Judge of the whole earth, he is the only One competent to measure the motivations of our hearts. In the Hebrew Scriptures, the word "judge" is often parallel to the word "king." When we pray to God our *Shophet* (sho-PHAIT), we are praying to the One whose righteousness demands perfect justice but who has also provided a way for us to be acquitted of our guilt through the life, death, and resurrection of his Son.

Key Scripture

Judgment will again be founded on righteousness,
    and all the upright in heart will follow it. (Psalm 94:15)

Monday

GOD REVEALS HIS NAME

Rise up, O Judge of the earth;
    pay back to the proud what they deserve.
How long will the wicked, O LORD,
    how long will the wicked be jubilant?
They pour out arrogant words;
    all the evildoers are full of boasting.
They crush your people, O LORD;
    they oppress your inheritance.
They slay the widow and the alien;
    they murder the fatherless.
They say, "The Lord does not see;
    the God of Jacob pays no heed."
Take heed, you senseless ones among the people;
    you fools, when will you become wise?
Does he who implanted the ear not hear?
    Does he who formed the eye not see?
Does he who disciplines nations not punish?
    Does he who teaches man lack knowledge?
The LORD knows the thoughts of man;
    he knows that they are futile.
Blessed is the man you discipline, O LORD,
    the man you teach from your law;
you grant him relief from days of trouble,
    till a pit is dug for the wicked.
For the LORD will not reject his people;
    he will never forsake his inheritance.
Judgment will again be founded on righteousness,
    and all the upright in heart will follow it.
        (Psalm 94:2–15)

Lord, you alone can judge the motivations of the heart. I pray that your justice will reign in my life and in all the nations of the earth. Bless those who long for justice. May they be satisfied.

Understanding the Name

The Hebrew verb *shapat* (sha-PHAT) can be translated in a variety of ways, including "judge," "govern," "vindicate," "decide," "defend," and "deliver." In the Hebrew Scriptures the word often combined the three primary functions of government—the executive, legislative, and judicial—that modern Western nations separate. That's why leaders like Gideon, Samson, and Deborah were called judges. When we read the word "judge" (*shophet*, sho-PHAIT) in the Hebrew Scriptures, we need to remember that it often connotes the broader meaning of "rule" or "ruler."

The prophets often chided Israel's rulers for failing to act justly, reserving their harshest words for those who ignored the rights of aliens, the poor, the fatherless, and the widow.

When the word "judge" is used in the New Testament, it tends to mirror the meaning of the word in Greek culture, emphasizing judicial functions rather than overall rule. The New Testament depicts Jesus as Judge of both the living and the dead.

Studying the Name

1. Who are the victims of injustice the psalmist names? How are such people still victimized in the world today?
2. What reason does the psalmist give for the brazenness of those who do evil? How does this perception of God shape our own world?
3. Contrast the fool and the wise person as described by the psalmist.
4. How have you experienced God's discipline in your life?
5. Why do you think justice is often something we have to wait for?

Tuesday

PRAYING THE NAME

Do not judge, or you too will be judged. For in the same way you judge others, you will be judged, and with the measure you use, it will be measured to you. (Matthew 7:1)

You, therefore, have no excuse, you who pass judgment on someone else, for at whatever point you judge the other, you are condemning yourself, because you who pass judgment do the same things. Now we know that God's judgment against those who do such things is based on truth. So when you, a mere man, pass judgment on them and yet do the same things, do you think you will escape God's judgment? Or do you show contempt for the riches of his kindness, tolerance and patience, not realizing that God's kindness leads you toward repentance? (Romans 2:1–4)

Reflect On: Matthew 7:1–5 and Romans 2:1–4
Praise God: Because he is perfectly just.
Offer Thanks: For God's ability to read our hearts.
Confess: Any tendency to judge the motivations of another's heart.
Ask God: To keep you from becoming critical and judgmental of others.

Have you ever felt unjustly accused of some offense, large or small, that you never committed? Several years ago, someone I knew fairly well started a campaign against me, painting me in a negative light to some of my closest friends. I felt hurt, bewildered, and angry, knowing that her accusations were false. It was a difficult situation to deal with especially since she always delivered her attacks with a velvet hammer, couching her comments in expressions of apparent concern. I tried confronting her, but she wouldn't admit that she was doing anything wrong.

During that time, the words of Psalm 43 took on a kind of personal urgency: "Vindicate me, O God, and plead my cause. . . . Send forth your light and your truth, let them guide me" (Psalm 43:1, 3). I prayed fervently and frequently that the truth would come out. But while I prayed, I noted an unhealthy feeling rising inside me, like mercury on a steamy August day. Who did this woman think she was? What made her think she could play "god" in other peoples' lives? Why was she so manipulative and judgmental? I found myself wishing I could special order a punishment just for her, one that would exactly duplicate my suffering.

Fortunately, the Holy Spirit brought me up short by revealing the precise nature of my feelings, calling them by names I could recognize: "bitterness" and a "desire for revenge." I knew that if I let them take their natural course, it wouldn't be long before "hatred" came waltzing around the corner. In that moment God gave me the grace to let go of my desire to judge my former friend for misjudging me. Instead of acting as judge, exposing her misdeeds and then sentencing her to a fitting punishment as I longed to do, I simply decided to forgive her. Whenever I felt tempted to wish her ill, I prayed that God would bless her. Before long I began to mean it, trusting that judgment belonged, not to me, but to God.

Since then, I have often thanked God for the grace I received at that time. Though I eventually felt vindicated, the real victory came not from escaping her unkind remarks but from evading the bitterness and resentment that threatened my heart.

Whether you are prone to being critical and judgmental or whether you have borne the brunt of that tendency in others, remember that even though we need to evaluate the actions of others, only God can judge the motivations of their hearts.

Wednesday

PRAYING THE NAME

Say among the nations, "The LORD reigns."
The world is firmly established, it cannot be moved;
he will judge the peoples with equity.
Let the heavens rejoice, let the earth be glad;
let the sea resound, and all that is in it;
let the fields be jubilant, and everything in them.
Then all the trees of the forest will sing for joy;
they will sing before the LORD, for he comes,
he comes to judge the earth.
He will judge the world in righteousness
and the peoples in his truth. (Psalm 96:10–13)

Reflect On: Psalm 96:10–13
Praise God: Because perfect justice is perfectly reflected in his character.
Offer Thanks: For God's promise to judge all people in his truth.
Confess: Any tendency to ignore the plight of the innocent.
Ask God: To help you recognize and counter injustice.

Most of us cringe a little when we hear that God is not only our Healer and Refuge, Savior and Shepherd, but also our Judge. Judgment, after all, doesn't mesh with our ideas of love and mercy. But what if you were Eddie Joe Lloyd, languishing in prison for seventeen years for a crime you didn't commit? Wouldn't you long for a little bit of that heavenly judgment to come your way? For God to shed light on your innocence and restore your freedom? That's exactly what happened on August 26, 2002, when Eddie walked out of court a free man after DNA evidence proved he did not rape and murder a sixteen-year-old girl in Detroit, Michigan, in 1984.

After the crime, police had interrogated Eddie while he was a patient in a mental hospital. During the course of these interrogations, one of the investigating officers suggested to Lloyd that by confessing and allowing himself to be arrested, Lloyd would help "smoke out" the real perpetrator. To make the confession convincing, the detective allegedly fed him details he couldn't have known about the crime. Eddie confessed to the crime and then later recanted. At the time of the trial, the presiding judge was so convinced of Eddie's guilt that he publicly lamented that the court did not have the power to sentence Eddie to death by hanging. Seventeen years later, incontrovertible evidence forced the same judge to free him, after Eddie had spent more than a third of his life in prison.

Sadly, injustice is an ever-present reality in our world. But rather than shrug it off as the inevitable consequence of life post-Eden, we should share the Lord's own indignation, noting that God reserves the harshest penalties for those who fail to uphold justice for the lowly of the earth—the mentally ill, minorities, orphans, widows, and the poor. The Bible calls them "the afflicted who have no one to help" (Psalm 72:12). As lovers of God, we should love his judgments and hunger for the day when his justice will be established over the entire earth.

Today take time to pray for those who have been wrongly accused and imprisoned for crimes they did not commit. Pray that God will bring the guilty to justice and set the innocent free.

Thursday

PRAYING THE NAME

Then I saw a great white throne and him who was seated on it. Earth and sky fled from his presence, and there was no place for them. And I saw the dead, great and small, standing before the throne, and books were opened. Another book was opened, which is the book of life. The dead were judged according to what they had done as recorded in the books. The sea gave up the dead that were in it, and death and Hades gave up the dead that were in them, and each person was judged according to what he had done. Then death and Hades were thrown into the lake of fire. The lake of fire is the second death. If anyone's name was not found written in the book of life, he was thrown into the lake of fire. (Revelation 20:11–15)

Reflect On: Revelation 20:11–15
Praise God: Who reigns over both the great and the small.
Offer Thanks: That God will one day destroy death's power over you.
Confess: Any complacency that prevents you from sharing your faith.
Ask God: To save those in your life who do not know him.

Jonathan Edwards in his sermon "Sinners in the Hands of an Angry God" struck terror in the hearts of his eighteenth-century listeners by assuring the unconverted that the bow of God's wrath was bent straight at their hearts and that nothing but the mere pleasure of an angry God kept "the arrow one moment from being made drunk with your blood." He spoke relentlessly of their danger, painting a graphic picture of "hell's wide gaping mouth" and of sinners hanging precariously over it like a spider or "some loathsome insect" about to be dropped into the fire. Their wickedness, he assured them, made them as "heavy as lead, and to tend downwards with great weight and pressure towards hell."

His sermon was so terrifying that people jumped out of their seats weeping and wailing over their sins, making such a commotion that Edwards was unable to finish. If it's possible to frighten people into heaven, Jonathan Edwards must certainly have done so through the words of what has become America's most famous and most controversial sermon.

While I wouldn't recommend handing out copies of that sermon to unconverted friends and family members, Edwards' words speak powerfully about a danger hardly anyone warns us of today. Hell, after all, has become passé. Even if people admit the possibility of such a place, they doubt that anyone they care about is heading in that direction. But Scripture assures us hell is more than a state of mind or the figment of an overactive religious imagination. The Bible describes it as a place of torment, of eternal separation from the God who made us. What, after all, could be more tormenting than to live forever without the slightest trace of God?

Sunshine, soft grass, the sound of laughter, the smell of food, the love of family and friends—these and a million other delights are blessings from the hand of God we tend to take for granted. Without his presence or his sustaining gifts, hell cannot hold a single pleasure, a moment's joy. Imagine living in utter loneliness, a howling emptiness, complete alienation, hating and being hated—world without end, forever and ever. The opposite of all we ever longed for, of everything we were made for.

In one sense the prospect of eternal judgment is supposed to scare us. Pondering hell and the reality of a godless eternity can propel us toward heaven, motivating us to live for God so fully that we attract others to him. It can invigorate our spiritual lives.

Let us pray today as though there is no tomorrow—especially for those who don't yet know God. Let us ask him to shake them up and wake them up and bring them home before it is too late.

Friday

PROMISES ASSOCIATED WITH GOD'S NAME

God's justice is tempered by his great mercy, which is most powerfully and eloquently expressed in the person of Jesus Christ. No matter what your life may have looked like before you came to Christ, there is no longer any condemnation for you. Today the Judge of the whole earth rises to show you compassion. Express your thanks by imitating his justice—feeding the hungry, welcoming the stranger, clothing the poor, visiting those who are in prison, and nursing the sick.

Promises in Scripture

Yet the LORD longs to be gracious to you;
he rises to show you compassion.
For the LORD is a God of justice.
Blessed are all who wait for him! (Isaiah 30:18)

I tell you the truth, whoever hears my word and believes him who sent me has eternal life and will not be condemned; he has crossed over from death to life. I tell you the truth, a time is coming and has now come when the dead will hear the voice of the Son of God and those who hear will live. For as the Father has life in himself, so he has granted the Son to have life in himself. And he has given him authority to judge because he is the Son of Man. (John 5:24–27)

Then the King will say to those on his right, "Come, you who are blessed by my Father; take your inheritance, the kingdom prepared for you since the creation of the world. For I was hungry and you gave me something to eat, I was thirsty and you gave me something to drink, I was a stranger and you invited me in, I needed clothes and you clothed me, I was sick and you looked after me, I was in prison and you came to visit me." (Matthew 25:34–36)

Continued Prayer and Praise

Pray for the leaders of your country. (Psalm 72:1–19)

Pray for God's judgment on oppressive rulers. (Psalm 94:1–15)

Pray that the Lord will establish his kingdom through his perfect justice. (Isaiah 11:1–9)

22

Hope of Israel

Miqweh Yisrael

The Name

Hope is the great stabilizer. It steadies us in times of fear and difficulty, not because we know that everything will turn out as we want, but because we know that God is trustworthy. Hope is what helps us stay on course regardless of circumstances. Biblical hope finds its roots in God and in his goodness, mercy, and power. We exercise our hope when we endure patiently. We nurture our hope when we read God's Word. Though we hope for earthly blessings, our greatest hope is aimed at the life to come, when God will not only wipe away our tears but invite us to share his joy forever. When you pray to *Miqweh Yisrael*, the Hope of Israel, you are praying to the One who saves all those who trust in him.

Key Scripture

A blessing on the man who puts his trust in the Lord,
    with the Lord for his hope.
He is like a tree by the waterside
    that thrusts its roots to the stream;
when the heat comes it feels no alarm,

its foliage stays green;
it has no worries in a year of drought,
and never ceases to bear fruit. . . .
Hope of Israel, Lord! (Jeremiah 17:7–8, 13 JB)

Monday

God Reveals His Name

A curse on the man who puts his trust in man,
    who relies on things of flesh,
    whose heart turns from the Lord.
He is like dry scrub in the wastelands:
    If good comes, he has no eyes for it,
He settles in the parched places of the wilderness,
    a salt land, uninhabited.
A blessing on the man who puts his trust in the Lord,
    with the Lord for his hope.
He is like a tree by the waterside
    that thrusts its roots to the stream;
when the heat comes it feels no alarm,
    its foliage stays green;
it has no worries in a year of drought,
    and never ceases to bear fruit. . . .
Hope of Israel, Lord!
Those who turn from you will be uprooted from
        the land,
    since they have abandoned the fountain of
        living water. (Jeremiah 17:5–8, 13 jb)

Lord, no eye has seen, no ear has heard, what you have prepared for those who love you. Thank you for all that you do, for all that you are, and for all that you promise. Help me to wait and to watch, to trust and believe. You are my hope and my strength. Amen.

Understanding the Name

In the Hebrew Scriptures, hope is often connected to the expectation that God is a deliverer who will save those who trust in him. It urges us to wait confidently for him to act. In the New Testament hope is rooted firmly in Jesus—in his life, death, and resurrection as well as in his coming again in glory. We can also have hope for this life because the Holy Spirit indwells us, re-creating the image of Christ within us. Biblical hope is a new kind of strength, enabling us to be patient and enduring regardless of what we face. *Miqweh Yisrael* (MIK-weh yis-ra-AIL), the Hope of Israel, he is the God who saves his people.

Studying the Name

1. What does it mean to put your trust in people? Give some examples.
2. What does it mean to put your hope in the Lord? How have you been able to hope in him?
3. How have you experienced God's provision? What can you do to root yourself more firmly in God?
4. Describe what you are hoping for in your life.

Tuesday

PRAYING THE NAME

A blessing on the man who puts his trust in the LORD,
with the LORD for his hope.
He is like a tree by the waterside
that thrusts its roots to the stream;
when the heat comes it feels no alarm,
its foliage stays green;
it has no worries in a year of drought,
and never ceases to bear fruit. . . .
Hope of Israel, LORD!
Those who turn from you will be uprooted from the land,
since they have abandoned the fountain of living
water. (Jeremiah 17:5–8, 13 JB)

Reflect On: Jeremiah 17:5–8, 13
Praise God: The fountain of living water.
Offer Thanks: For the ways God has already rewarded your hope.
Confess: Any lack of belief in God's self-description provided by Scripture.
Ask God: To help you root your life fully in him.

Grey Is the Color of Hope is the title of a book by Irina Ratushinkaya, a poet who was unjustly imprisoned in the Soviet Union during the 1980s. With all due respect, it would also make a great title for a book about life in Michigan during the long winter months. I remember one January a few years back, when the total sunlight for the month was measured neither in terms of days or hours but in terms of mere minutes—eight to be precise. If you weren't lucky enough to be looking out a window when the sun finally broke through the clouds, you would have missed it. Little wonder my five-year-old stood at the front door a few days ago and started jumping up and down, clapping and squealing excitedly: "The sun, the sun, the sun!" You know it's bad when a preschooler starts acting like that.

And then there's my mother. Her way of dealing with the endless gray skies is to pretend they aren't so endless and so gray. She insists on wearing her sunglasses on the cloudiest of days because "it's so bright out." She sees "gray," not as a shade descending into black, but as a color that's on its way to becoming light.

Maybe that's how we should think about our lives during periods that seem unremittingly gray or dark. Instead of letting anxiety or doubt paint the darkest possible conclusion to our problems, we need to stoke our hope, to let it advance against the shadows until the darkness recedes. "'For I know the plans I have for you,' declares the LORD, 'plans to prosper you and not to harm you, plans to give you hope and a future'" (Jeremiah 29:11).

Hope grows best in the soil of faithfulness. As we live our lives for God, loving his law, doing his will, immersing ourselves in his Word, believing he is who he says he is, and worshiping him together with his people, our hope will grow stronger, and we will be like the tree planted by water, whose leaves are always green and supple. We will also experience the truth of the words of the prophet Isaiah, who assured us that:

those who hope in the LORD
will renew their strength.
They will soar on wings like eagles;
they will run and not grow weary,
they will walk and not be faint. (Isaiah 40:31)

Pray the words of Jeremiah 17:5–8. Then close your eyes and imagine that you are a tree whose roots go down to the stream. Ask God to nourish your hope and renew your strength.

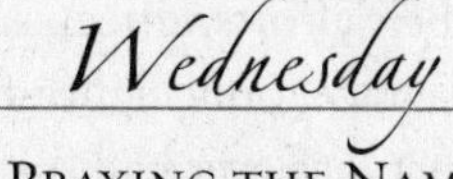

Wednesday

PRAYING THE NAME

We have this hope as an anchor for the soul, firm and secure. (Hebrews 6:19)

Therefore we will not fear, though the earth give way
and the mountains fall into the heart of the sea,
though its waters roar and foam
and the mountains quake with their surging.
(Psalm 46:2–3)

Reflect On: Hebrews 6:19 and Psalm 46:2–3
Praise God: Who is unchanging.
Offer Thanks: For his unchanging strength, love, and protection.
Confess: Any tendency to put your hope in things that cannot save you.
Ask God: To show you how to anchor your soul in him.

The Fastnet Race is one of the toughest and most prestigious offshore races in the world, capping a series of five races that make up the coveted Admiral's Cup. On August 11, 1979, 303 yachts embarked from the Isle of Wight in the English Channel, each crew having the same goal—to be the fastest yacht in the 608-mile race.

Saturday, the first day of the race, was picture perfect—sunny with a pleasant breeze. But by lunchtime on Monday savage winds began whipping the Irish Sea into a fury. That night, force 10 winds created walls of water 35–40 feet high. For twenty hours 2,500 men and women battled the raging winds, their boats tossed about like toys in the tumultuous sea.

After receiving a string of mayday calls, British and Irish naval vessels, a Dutch frigate, helicopters, and several lifeboats came to the rescue. But despite their efforts, fifteen sailors perished. Of the 303 yachts that began the race, only eighty-five made it to the finish line. The largest Fastnet race ever had turned into the worst disaster in yachting history.

The lessons learned from Fastnet are many, but there are two that stand out. First, experienced sailors now realize it is best to stay with the boat no matter what. The Fastnet sailors who did stay with their boats survived while many of those who took to life rafts died. Lifeboats should have been a last resort. Second, a sea anchor or a set of drogues (drag devices used to steady a boat in high seas) can help a boat weather a violent storm by enabling its helmsman to maintain control. In the Fastnet tragedy, only one drag device was used and the boat using it survived. Several boats were abandoned because of conditions a sea anchor could have alleviated—loss of rudders, intolerable motion below decks, dismastings, and capsizing.

But what does a sailing disaster have to do with one of God's titles—the Hope of Israel? Simply this—for two millennia the Christian symbol for hope has been an anchor. What better way to picture the One who is utterly reliable, completely steady, invulnerable to all the forces of evil that threaten us? If our hope is grounded in God, we will not be destroyed when gale force winds begin to blow in our direction, when fear, pain, grief, and disappointment threaten to overwhelm us. No matter how terrible the storm, we can survive because God is with us.

Sometimes, however, we let fear take over. The conditions we face seem so impossible that we are tempted to jump ship. Instead of clinging to God, we jump into "lifeboats" of our own making, things that promise security but don't deliver it—wealth, hard work, brains, alcohol, relationships, food. Rely on any of these long enough and you will find how incapable they are of keeping you safe in the midst of real trouble. Misplaced hopes are dangerous because they keep us from anchoring ourselves in God, the only one who can save us. No wonder the hymnist Isaac Watts penned these words to a song still sung by millions:

O God, our help in ages past,
Our hope for years to come,
Our shelter from the stormy blast,
And our eternal home.

Thursday

PRAYING THE NAME

Though he slay me, yet will I hope in him. (Job 13:15)

My soul waits for the Lord
more than watchmen wait for the morning,
more than watchmen wait for the morning.
O Israel, put your hope in the LORD,
for with the LORD is unfailing love
and with him is full redemption. (Psalm 130:6–7)

Reflect On:	Job 13:15 and Psalm 130:6–7
Praise God:	For his unfailing love.
Offer Thanks:	For the gift of hope.
Confess:	Any tendency toward hopelessness.
Ask God:	To show you how to bring your mind into alignment with his truth.

Antismoking campaigns have been enormously successful over the last thirty years, painting cigarette smoking as dangerous, dirty, and disgusting—the nastiest of habits with the nastiest of consequences. But there's another silent killer on the prowl that few people are warning against. Taking a cue from the antitobacco campaign, the warning we need to hear today is this: "Caution, Hopelessness May Be Hazardous to Your Health."

That's the conclusion of numerous clinical studies showing a direct link between feelings of hopelessness and the incidence of diseases like hypertension, coronary disease, and cancer. In fact, chronically high levels of hopelessness may lead to premature death. In one study of eight hundred elderly Americans funded by the National Institute on Aging, participants were asked to answer this question: "Are you hopeful about the future?" Those who responded "no" were classified as hopeless. Then the participants were tracked for the next three to seven years. Of those classified as "hopeless," 29 percent died compared with only 11 percent of those classified as "hopeful."

Though a variety of factors may be at work when it comes to linking hopelessness and illness, it is possible that feelings of hopelessness may lead to biochemical changes that weaken our immune systems. Just as hopelessness weakens our bodies, it can also damage our souls. Hope, by contrast, is a tonic for both body and soul.

One of my favorite definitions of hope comes from writer and playwright Jean Kerr: "Hope is the feeling you have that the feeling you have isn't permanent." But the biblical notion of hope is far sturdier. For one thing, biblical hope is not merely a matter of emotions. It doesn't involve pumping ourselves up or mere wishful thinking. Nor does it depend on circumstances. Instead, it is deeply rooted in our relationship with God, who is the repository of our hope.

Hope gives us the steady confidence that God is working for our good in all things, as Paul tells us in Romans 8:28. And *all* means *all.* Illness, emotional problems, failure, hardship, betrayal, calamity, financial ruin, even death—nothing can ultimately swallow our hope. We may at times feel disappointed, depressed, afraid, sad, or confused, but we will never give way to despair. Hope gives us supernatural staying power so that we can endure until the day God fulfills the greatest of all his promises—inviting us to spend the rest of our lives forever in his presence.

That's where true hope will lead you if you let it.

Friday

PROMISES ASSOCIATED WITH GOD'S NAME

A few years ago a friend of mine was diagnosed with late stage colon cancer. There was nothing that could be done for her medically. But Judy was a woman of boundless hope, who was certain God meant to heal her. She prayed and many people prayed for her. She took good care of herself and tried alternative medical approaches, hoping for a cure. She read books that increased her hope and her faith. She had a powerful will to live.

During the course of her ordeal, her faith so buoyed mine that it seemed as though she were the one encouraging me rather than the other way around. About two weeks before she died, I stopped by to see her. Judy came to the door with her mother. I held in my hand a just published copy of a book I had written and dedicated to her. It was a bittersweet moment. I can still see the two of them standing arm in arm on that sunny fall morning, mother and daughter smiling as tears coursed down their cheeks.

I cannot get their faces out of my mind. They captured for me the meaning of hope, because hope isn't false. It doesn't pretend away our sorrow but rises up inside it. It's a brightness that can't be quenched, a gift for this life that's meant to carry us into the next.

Promises in Scripture

But the eyes of the LORD are on those who fear him,
on those whose hope is in his unfailing love. (Psalm 33:18)

But those who hope in the LORD
will renew their strength. (Isaiah 40:31)

I tell you the truth, you will weep and mourn while the world rejoices. You will grieve, but your grief will turn to joy. A woman giving birth to a child has pain because her time has come; but when her baby is born she forgets the anguish because of her joy that a child is born into the world. So with you: Now is your time of grief, but I will see you again and you will rejoice, and no one will take away your joy. (John 16:20–22)

Therefore my heart is glad and my tongue rejoices;
my body also will live in hope,
because you will not abandon me to the grave,
nor will you let your Holy One see decay.
You have made known to me the paths of life;
you will fill me with joy in your presence. (Acts 2:26–28; quoted from Psalm 16:9–11)

Continued Prayer and Praise

Hope in God and you will not be put to shame. (Psalm 25:2–5; Jeremiah 14:8)

Wait in hope for the Lord. (Psalm 33:16–22)

Hope in God's name. (Psalm 52:8–9)

Place your hope in God's Word. (Psalm 119:81)

Thank God because his compassions do not fail. (Lamentations 3:21–23)

Remember that hope does not disappoint us. (Romans 5:1–5)

Praise God because nothing can separate us from his love. (Romans 8:28–38)

Hope in Jesus. (1 Timothy 1:1; Titus 2:11–14)

23

The Lord Our Righteousness

יהוה צִדְקֵנוּ

Yahweh Tsidqenu

The Name

Righteousness isn't a popular word in our culture. Yet righteousness is essential to our happiness because it involves being in right relationship or right standing with God and conforming to his character, fulfilling our responsibilities toward him and others. But righteousness is impossible for us to achieve, no matter how much we might long for it. It comes only as God's gift to us through faith in his Son. When we pray to the Lord Our Righteousness, we are praying to the One who has intervened on our behalf to restore us to his likeness and therefore to fellowship with himself.

Key Scripture

In his days Judah will be saved
    and Israel will live in safety.
This is the name by which he will be called:
    The LORD Our Righteousness. (Jeremiah 23:6)

Monday

GOD REVEALS HIS NAME

"The days are coming," declares the LORD,
 "when I will raise up to David a righteous Branch,
a King who will reign wisely
 and do what is just and right in the land.
In his days Judah will be saved
 and Israel will live in safety.
This is the name by which he will be called:
 The LORD Our Righteousness....
"This is the covenant I will make with the house of
Israel
 after that time," declares the LORD.
"I will put my law in their minds
 and write it on their hearts.
I will be their God,
 and they will be my people."
  (Jeremiah 23:5–6; 31:33)

But now a righteousness from God, apart from law, has been made known, to which the Law and the Prophets testify. This righteousness from God comes through faith in Jesus Christ to all who believe. There is no difference, for all have sinned and fall short of the glory of God, and are justified freely by his grace through the redemption that came by Christ Jesus. God presented him as a sacrifice of atonement, through faith in his blood. (Romans 3:21–25a)

Father, I admit that I have sinned and fallen far short of your glory—of your purity, your justice, your integrity, your mercy, and your love. I have no right to stand in your presence, except by the grace of your Son through his offering of love on the cross. Thank you, God, for drawing me back when I was so far away. Help me to hunger and thirst for righteousness on this earth—that all men and women might return to you and give you glory through the love and power and mercy of your Son, Jesus Christ. Amen.

Understanding the Name

The Hebrew word *tsedeq* is usually translated as "righteousness" but can also be translated as "righteous," "honest," "right," "justice," "accurate," "just," "truth," or "integrity." Righteousness primarily involves being in right standing with God. As such it concerns fulfilling the demands of relationship with both God and with others. Though people were often called righteous in the Hebrew Scriptures if they observed the Law, Jesus and the writers of the New Testament stress that righteousness is not merely a matter of outward behavior but a matter of the heart—of thoughts, motives, and desires. The goal is not merely to *do* what God says but to *become* like him. In the words of Addison Leitch, righteousness "is primarily and basically a relationship, never an attainment. . . . Christian righteousness . . . is a direction, a loyalty, a commitment, a hope—and only someday an arrival."

The prophet Jeremiah predicted the coming of a King who would be called "The LORD Our Righteousness" (yah-WEH tsid-KAY-nu). Jesus fulfilled this prophecy by restoring our relationship with God through his life, death, and resurrection. Paul proclaims in his letter to the Romans, "But now a righteousness from God, apart from law, has been made known, to which the Law and the Prophets testify. This righteousness from God comes through faith in Jesus Christ to all who believe" (Romans 3:21–22).

Studying the Name

1. Jeremiah reveals that the coming King will be known as "The LORD Our Righteousness." What comes to mind when you hear the words "righteous" or "righteousness"?

2. What does it mean to have God's law written on your heart?
3. How do you think Jesus' sacrifice has affected your relationship with God?
4. What do you think it means to have "faith in his blood"?

Tuesday

Praying the Name

There is no one righteous, not even one. (Romans 3:10)

Blessed are those who hunger and thirst for righteousness, for they will be filled. (Matthew 5:6)

Reflect On: Romans 3:10; Matthew 5:6
Praise God: For his absolute integrity.
Offer Thanks: That God does not abandon us to the power of sin.
Confess: Any apathy about living a righteous life.
Ask God: To show you the depth of your need for him.

The word "righteous" isn't a word you're likely to hear at work, at home, on public radio, or network TV. Though it may conjure images of the popular singing duo the Righteous Brothers (at least to the over-forty crowd), it is far likelier to make us think of religious prigs, people who alienate us with their smug, self-satisfied views.

But the Bible speaks of righteousness as something altogether different from self-righteousness. To be righteous is to be in a right relationship with God and with others. Rather than suffering the misshaping power of sin, the righteous bear a striking resemblance to God, not in terms of his power but in terms of his character. They display his faithful love, his mercy, humility, integrity, and justice. Furthermore, the Bible states that God hears the prayers of the righteous. He blesses their homes, smooths their paths, grants their desires, rescues them from trouble, and makes them prosper. But here's the rub: Scripture also says that God is the only One who is completely righteous.

This truth came home to me recently while I was praying for someone who seems far from God. That's when I read these words from John Henry Newman: "For it is in proportion as we search our hearts and understand our own nature . . . in proportion as we comprehend the nature of disobedience and our actual sinfulness, that we feel what is the blessing of the removal of sin, redemption, pardon, sanctification, which otherwise are mere words." It suddenly occurred to me that I should pray not only for this young woman to know the love of Christ but also for her to know the state of her own heart so that she could recognize the depth of her need. How could she ever find her way home if she didn't even know she was lost?

Let us today prepare the way of the Lord by asking him to make us and those we pray for hungry and thirsty for righteousness. The righteousness God bestows through faith in his Son is the path to re-creating paradise, to gaining heaven, to enjoying the unbroken fellowship with God and each other that our Creator intended since the world's beginning.

Wednesday

PRAYING THE NAME

So the LORD said to him [Abram], "Bring me a heifer, a goat and a ram, each three years old, along with a dove and a young pigeon."

Abram brought all these to him, cut them in two and arranged the halves opposite each other; the birds, however, he did not cut in half. Then birds of prey came down on the carcasses, but Abram drove them away.

As the sun was setting, Abram fell into a deep sleep, and a thick and dreadful darkness came over him. . . . When the sun had set and darkness had fallen, a smoking firepot with a blazing torch appeared and passed between the pieces. (Genesis 15:9–12, 17)

He himself bore our sins in his body on the tree, so that we might die to sins and live for righteousness; by his wounds you have been healed. For you were like sheep going astray, but now you have returned to the Shepherd and Overseer of your souls. (1 Peter 2:24)

Reflect On: Genesis 15 and 1 Peter 2:24
Praise God: For his righteousness.
Offer Thanks: That God came seeking you.
Confess: Any tendency to forget what Jesus suffered for your sake.
Ask God: To increase your understanding of what Jesus has done for you.

Imagine sealing an agreement flanked not by lawyers who stand ready to witness your signature on a contract but by pieces of slaughtered animals that form an aisle you are to walk through. By taking part in this ancient ceremony and walking down that aisle, you are essentially saying, "May the same thing happen to me if I ever break my oath." That's precisely how God solemnized his covenant with Abraham. But the funny thing was, Abraham never walked down that aisle. Only God did, in the figure of the smoking firepot in Abraham's dream.

In the years that followed, God kept his part of the covenant while Abraham's descendants broke it on a regular basis. Instead of living in the shelter of their righteous God, they worshiped idols. Ignoring the Law, which was meant to lead them to their greatest happiness, they strayed until they could not find a way back. Still God came seeking them, ever faithful to the covenant he had made. He sent prophets to cry out to them; he afflicted them in an effort to bring them back; and he blessed them whenever they returned. But nothing worked for long. Israel's sin against a holy God called down the ancient curse.

But instead of tearing the oath-breakers apart in accordance with the ancient rite, God himself took the brunt of the struggle against evil, absorbing the punishment in the body of his Son, slaughtered on a cross. Jesus, Son of God and Son of Man, suffered the punishment we deserve. He was wounded for our transgressions, restoring us forever to the God who loves us.

Thank God today for his love and mercy, which like his justice is a part of his righteousness. Accept by faith the righteousness that comes to you through Jesus Christ, the one we call *Yahweh Tsidqenu*, The Lord Our Righteousness.

Thursday

PRAYING THE NAME

Then the LORD spoke to Job out of the storm:
"Brace yourself like a man;
I will question you,
and you shall answer me.
Would you discredit my justice?
Would you condemn me to justify yourself?" . . .
Then Job replied to the LORD . . .
"My ears had heard of you
but now my eyes have seen you.
Therefore I despise myself
and repent in dust and ashes."
(Job 40:7–8; 42:1, 5–6)

Reflect On: Job 40 and 42
Praise God: For his sovereignty.
Offer Thanks: For God's faithfulness to you.
Confess: Any tendency to accuse God of being unjust.
Ask God: To help you trust him in good times and bad.

The book of Job tells the story of a righteous man suddenly stripped of every earthly blessing—family, possessions, health. His losses came driving toward him in a loud, staccato beat—

"Job, your animals have been stolen!" someone shouted.

"All the servants have been murdered!" a man cried.

"Your children are dead!" a messenger screamed.

Job's suffering was immense, beyond imagining. After listening to the "theologically correct" but ultimately flawed advice of friends accusing him of hidden guilt for which he was being punished, Job became so disheartened that he accused God of gross injustice.

At the end of the story, Job received not answers but a vision of God so profound, so dazzling that by comparison he despised himself and repented "in dust and ashes." Then God proceeded to vindicate Job, blessing the latter part of his life more than the former.

To the question, "Why do good people suffer?" the book of Job provides no neat theological answer except to say that God has reasons for allowing the righteous to suffer that we may never understand. Our job is not to treat justice as a mathematical equation that can easily be solved in this world but to trust God to ultimately act with justice and mercy, consistent with his righteousness.

Today, pray for people you know who are suffering. Don't offer them easy answers or advice. But do listen to their complaints. Ask God to vindicate the innocent and comfort the righteous with a sense of his presence.

Friday

PROMISES ASSOCIATED WITH GOD'S NAME

Do you want to be rescued from trouble, to be prosperous, safe, and a blessing to others? Do you want to be crowned with God's blessings? Do you want God to answer your prayers? These are just some of the fruits that come from living a righteous life as described in the book of Proverbs. To pursue righteousness is to pursue God himself through faith in his Son, Jesus, who promised, "Blessed are those who hunger and thirst for righteousness, for they will be filled" (Matthew 5:6).

Promises in Scripture

Blessings crown the head of the righteous. (Proverbs 10:6)

The memory of the righteous will be a blessing. (Proverbs 10:7)

The mouth of the righteous is a fountain of life. (Proverbs 10:11)

The lips of the righteous nourish many. (Proverbs 10:21)

What the wicked dread will come upon them,
but the desire of the righteous will be granted. (Proverbs 10:24 NRSV)

When the storm has swept by, the wicked are gone,
but the righteous stand firm forever. (Proverbs 10:25)

The righteous are delivered from trouble,
and the wicked get into it instead. (Proverbs 11:8 NRSV)

Prosperity is the reward of the righteous. (Proverbs 13:21)

Continued Prayer and Praise

Ask God to give you a new heart, removing your heart of stone. (Ezekiel 36:26–28)

Ask God to guide you in paths of righteousness for his name's sake. (Psalm 23:2–3)

Remember that righteousness from God comes through faith. (Romans 3:10–31)

Ask God for the grace to pursue a life of righteousness. (1 Timothy 6:6–12)

24

God Most High

El Elyon

The Name

When applied to God, the term *Elyon*, meaning "Highest" or "Exalted One," emphasizes that God is the highest in every realm of life. In the New Testament, Jesus is known as the Son of the Most High while the Holy Spirit is the power of the Most High. All who belong to Christ are revealed as sons and daughters of the Most High by imitating the Father in heaven. When you praise the Most High, you are worshiping the One whose power, mercy, and sovereignty cannot be matched.

Key Scripture

When that period was over, I, Nebuchadnezzar, lifted my eyes to heaven, and my reason returned to me.
I blessed the Most High,
    and praised and honored the one who lives forever.
For his sovereignty is an everlasting sovereignty,
    and his kingdom endures from generation to generation.
(Daniel 4:34 NRSV)

Monday

God Reveals His Name

Belteshazzar [Daniel] answered [King Nebuchadnezzar], "My lord, may the dream be for those who hate you, and its interpretation for your enemies! . . . This is the interpretation, O king, and it is a decree of the Most High that has come upon my lord the king: You shall be driven away from human society, and your dwelling shall be with the wild animals. You shall be made to eat grass like oxen, you shall be bathed with the dew of heaven, and seven times shall pass over you, until you have learned that the Most High has sovereignty over the kingdom of mortals, and gives it to whom he will. As it was commanded to leave the stump and roots of the tree, your kingdom shall be re-established for you from the time that you learn that Heaven is sovereign. Therefore, O king, may my counsel be acceptable to you: atone for your sins with righteousness, and your iniquities with mercy to the oppressed, so that your prosperity may be prolonged."

All this came upon King Nebuchadnezzar. At the end of twelve months he was walking on the roof of the royal palace of Babylon, and the king said, "Is this not magnificent Babylon, which I have built as a royal capital by my mighty power and for my glorious majesty?" While the words were still in the king's mouth, a voice came from heaven: "O King Nebuchadnezzar, to you it is declared: The kingdom has departed from you! You shall be driven away from human society, and your dwelling shall be with the animals of the field. You shall be made to eat grass like oxen, and seven times shall pass over you, until you have learned that the Most High has sovereignty over the kingdom of mortals and gives it to whom he will." Immediately the sentence was fulfilled against Nebuchadnezzar. He was driven away from human society, ate grass like oxen, and his body was bathed with the dew of heaven, until his hair grew as long as eagles' feathers and his nails became like birds' claws.

When that period was over, I, Nebuchadnezzar, lifted my eyes to heaven, and my reason returned to me.

> I blessed the Most High,
> and praised and honored the one who lives forever.
> For his sovereignty is an everlasting sovereignty,
> and his kingdom endures from generation to generation. (Daniel 4:19, 24–34 NRSV)

El Elyon, you are God above all gods, the One who rules over the rulers of the earth. May every knee bow to you and every tongue confess that you are Lord forever. Amen.

Understanding the Name

Elyon, the title given to the highest of the Canaanite gods, was appropriated by the Hebrews as a title for *Yahweh.* Emphasizing God's transcendence, the name *El Elyon* (EL el-YOHN) is first used in relation to Melchizedek, the king of Salem, who was also called "priest of God Most High" and who blessed Abraham in the name of "God Most High" (Genesis 14:18–20). The passage in Daniel regarding the interpretation of a dream that King Nebuchadnezzar had illustrates what happens when human beings forget who is highest in heaven and on earth. In Daniel, the Aramaic word *Illaya* is the equivalent of the Hebrew *El Elyon* and is translated as "God Most High."

Studying the Name

1. What does the king's dream and Daniel's interpretation indicate about the source of Nebuchadnezzar's greatness and prosperity?
2. Nebuchadnezzar may have been stricken by a rare form of insanity in which a human being believes he is a particular kind

of animal. Why do you think his boasting led to this kind of punishment?

3. What does Nebuchadnezzar's story reveal about the link between sanity and humility?
4. How have you been tempted to take credit for God's blessings?
5. What can you do to acknowledge God's greatness?

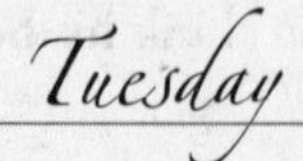

Praying the Name

For you, O Lord, are the Most High over all the earth;
you are exalted far above all gods. (Psalm 97:9)

Reflect On: Psalm 97
Praise God: For he is exalted far above all gods.
Offer Thanks: Because the God of all the earth has revealed himself to you.
Confess: Any overemphasis on pleasure or comfort in your life.
Ask God: To sharpen his image in your soul.

Psalm 97 paints a powerful picture of the Most High. A God so awesome that mountains melt before him! So magnificent that the earth trembles in his presence! A God above everything and everyone! The psalmist's words made me wonder how different my life would be if I could etch this vision into my soul. How could I take my eyes off such a God? Wouldn't this picture of him dominate my thoughts? Wouldn't it compel my devotion and reshape my response to life, moment by moment, day after day?

Wondering why I find it hard to keep God's majesty in view, it occurred to me to wonder what really was "most high" in my life. What had I been paying most attention to lately—thinking about, dreaming about, desiring? Was it God—or something else? The truth pricked. Hadn't I been spending an awful lot of time envisioning that little cottage near the beach I wanted? Dreaming about those gorgeous sunsets and the sand beneath my feet? Plotting and scheming to make it a reality? Sadly, I realized that earthly pleasures meant to bless had crept in, dulling my appetite for God.

I began to wonder what other pleasure-seeking habits were at work in me to displace God. How soft had I become? Was I in danger of developing what I call "spiritual cataracts"? Had my soul become so clouded by everything *but* God that I could only catch an occasional glimpse of him? What needed to change so that I could put the focus back where it belonged?

Perhaps you live as I do in a land of plenty. If so, ask yourself whether the good things of this life may be clouding your vision of who God is. Start by identifying what or who is "most high" in your own mind and heart. Is it God or something else—a relationship, a job, plans for your children, a dream for your future? If you find that your love for God has been edged out by lesser things, join me in begging God's forgiveness and asking for his mercy. Ask him to show you how to make him "Most High" in your heart as he is Most High in heaven and on earth.

Wednesday

Praying the Name

But love your enemies, do good, and lend, expecting nothing in return. Your reward will be great, and you will be children of the Most High; for he is kind to the ungrateful and the wicked. Be merciful, just as your Father is merciful. (Luke 6:35–36 NRSV)

Reflect On:	Luke 6:27–36
Praise God:	For his all-surpassing goodness.
Offer Thanks:	For the ways God has shown you mercy.
Confess:	Any pride that would keep you from modeling God's character.
Ask God:	For the grace to display God's character to those who don't deserve it.

Convicted sniper John Allen Muhammed, suspected of killing thirteen people and wounding six more, purportedly left a tarot card inscribed with the message "I am God" at the scene of one of the shootings in the Washington, D.C., area.

Just who, you may wonder, does the sniper think God is? His definition of God strikes us as obscene, as though God and power are an exact equation. But when you take power and subtract from it goodness, kindness, justice, and mercy, you get a monster, not God. Perhaps it is not surprising, as Elmer Towns suggests, that demons identified Jesus as the Son of the Most High on more than one occasion. Because being "Most High" in terms of power is what Satan has been after all along. He wants to rule and dominate, to destroy and kill. His lust for absolute power is what absolutely defines him.

But look at how Jesus defined "Most High." He told anyone who wanted to become a "child of the Most High" to be kind and merciful, to act as though they were "most low"—loving their enemies, doing good to them, lending without expecting anything back, treating the worst kind of people as though they were the best kind of people. He also instructed his disciples that whoever exalts himself will be humbled and whoever humbles himself will be exalted.

Today, ask for the grace to grow in the character of the Most High so that you will become a recognizable member of his family. Then praise him for who he is—Most High in power, Most High in mercy, Most High in goodness, and Most High in love.

Thursday

PRAYING THE NAME

Do not be afraid, Mary, you have found favor with God. You will be with child and give birth to a son, and you are to give him the name Jesus. He will be great and will be called the Son of the Most High. (Luke 1:30–32)

The Son is the radiance of God's glory and the exact representation of his being, sustaining all things by his powerful word. After he had provided purification for sins, he sat down at the right hand of the Majesty in heaven. So he became as much superior to the angels as the name he has inherited is superior to theirs. (Hebrew 1:3–4)

Reflect On: Acts 1:1–11 and Hebrews 1:3–4
Praise God: Because he reigns above all.
Offer Thanks: That your life is hidden in Christ.
Confess: Any tendency to live as though there's no such place as heaven.
Ask God: To help you set your heart on the things that are above, where Christ is.

Several years ago, a book titled *All I Really Need to Know I Learned in Kindergarten* stormed the bestseller lists. But ever since my eldest entered elementary school, I have had the opposite experience. Take first-grade science. I don't remember studying the solar system in grade school, let alone in first grade. But then again we didn't have stunning photographs from the Hubble Telescope to pique our curiosity. Still, it's embarrassing to hear yourself saying, "I didn't know that!" every time your six-year-old comes out with statements like, "Mom, did you know that outer space starts sixty miles above the earth?" Or, "Did you know that the sun is so high it would take a car 177 years to reach it going sixty miles an hour?" Or, "Did you know that Pluto is almost three billion miles away?"

"No, I humbly confess, I didn't know that."

But when it comes to celestial measurements, I do know one thing. Jesus—the radiance of God's glory and the exact representation of his being—is immeasurably higher than anything or anyone in this vast and beautiful universe.

Scripture tells us that after the resurrection, the Lord spent forty days on earth. When it was time to leave, he ascended to a place that is higher by far than any we can imagine. Did you know that when Jesus rose from the Mount of Olives, he didn't leave his human nature behind but instead took it straight up to heaven? John Chrysostom, the famous golden-mouthed preacher, says that angels looked on at the Ascension because they wanted "to see the unheard of spectacle of man appearing in heaven." He went on to say:

> Today we are raised up into heaven, we who seemed even unworthy of earth. We are exalted above the heavens; we arrive at the kingly throne. . . . Was it not enough to be elevated above the heavens? Was not such a glory beyond all expression? But He rose above the angels, He passed the Cherubim, He went higher than the Seraphim, He bypassed the Thrones, He did not stop until He arrived at the very throne of God.

Jesus, the Son of the Most High, reigning in heaven, remains both human and divine. Knowing this, let us cherish the words of Paul: "Since, then, you have been raised with Christ, set your hearts on things above, where Christ is seated at the right hand of God. Set your minds on things above, not on earthly things. For you died, and your life is now hidden with Christ in God. When Christ, who is your life, appears, then you also will appear with him in glory" (Colossians 3:1–4).

Friday

Promises Associated with God's Name

What threatens you? Financial insecurity, ill health, a difficult job, a troubled marriage? No matter how high your problems mount, God is higher still. No difficulty is beyond his reach. But what does it mean to take refuge in the Most High? Doesn't it mean to do at least four things—to pray, to repent, to obey, and to believe—and to do them on a regular basis? If you make these your lifelong habits, you will always stay close to God. And you will know the rest and peace that comes from living in the shadow of the God for whom nothing is impossible.

Promises in Scripture

I cry out to God Most High, to God,
who fulfills his purpose for me. (Psalm 57:2)

He who dwells in the shelter of the Most High
will rest in the shadow of the Almighty.
I will say of the Lord, "He is my refuge and my fortress,
my God, in whom I trust."
Surely he will save you from the fowler's snare
and from the deadly pestilence.
He will cover you with his feathers,
and under his wings you will find refuge;
his faithfulness will be your shield and rampart. . . .
If you make the Most High your dwelling—
even the Lord, who is my refuge—
then no harm will befall you,
no disaster will come near your tent. (Psalm 91:1–4, 9–10)

Continued Prayer and Praise

Remember that life and death, victory and failure are in the hands of the Most High. (Isaiah 2:6–10)

Thank God that his ways are higher than ours. (Isaiah 55:8–9)

Let the Most High be your shield. (Psalm 7:10)

Praise the Most High morning and night. (Psalm 92:1–3)

Consider the works of the Most High. (Psalm 107)

Praise Jesus, who is seated at the right hand of God. (Hebrews 1:3–4)

25

The Lord Is There

Yahweh Shammah

The Name

Strictly speaking, *Yahweh Shammah* is a name for a city rather than a title of God. But it is so closely associated with God's presence and power that it has often been equated with a name for God, at least in popular parlance. The name in the New Testament that is most closely associated with it is *Immanuel*, "God with us," a name that was given to Jesus. *Yahweh Shammah* (yah-WEH SHAM-mah), "The Lord is there," reminds us that we were created both to enjoy and to manifest God's presence.

Key Scripture

And the name of the city from that time on will be:
THE LORD IS THERE. (Ezekiel 48:35)

Monday

God Reveals His Name

I will gather them from all around and bring them back into their own land. I will make them one nation in the land, on the mountains of Israel. There will be one king over all of them and they will never again be two nations or be divided into two kingdoms. They will no longer defile themselves with their idols and vile images or with any of their offenses, for I will save them from all their sinful backsliding, and I will cleanse them. They will be my people, and I will be their God.

My servant David will be king over them, and they will all have one shepherd. They will follow my laws and be careful to keep my decrees. They will live in the land I gave to my servant Jacob, the land where your fathers lived. They and their children and their children's children will live there forever, and David my servant will be their prince forever. I will make a covenant of peace with them; it will be an everlasting covenant. I will establish them and increase their numbers, and I will put my sanctuary among them forever. My dwelling place will be with them; I will be their God, and they will be my people. Then the nations will know that I the Lord make Israel holy, when my sanctuary is among them forever. . . .

And the name of the city from that time on will be:

THE LORD IS THERE. (Ezekiel 37:21–28; 48:35)

Lord, arise and come to your resting place. Let your glory dwell with your people. Hear from heaven and forgive our sins. Lead us and guide us. Fill us with your presence by the power of your Spirit. May your eyes and your heart always be upon us. Establish your sanctuary among us forever. Amen.

Understanding the Name

Genesis is the story of beginnings. For a short while, it portrays an easy intimacy between God and the man and woman he made. But as soon as sin enters the picture, that intimacy is destroyed. Sensing that sin has rendered them unfit for God's presence, Adam and Eve try to hide. But God finds them and casts them out of paradise, barring the way back.

Nevertheless, he doesn't entirely abandon sinful humanity. Instead God begins to reestablish his relationship with them. He starts by choosing a people for his own. Then he delivers his people from their slavery in Egypt, as Deuteronomy 4:37 says, "by his *Presence* and his great strength." God dwells with his people first in the form of a pillar of cloud and fire, then in the movable tabernacle in the wilderness, and later in the Jerusalem temple.

But still God's people sin. Tragically, the prophet Ezekiel witnesses the glory of God departing from the temple because of their continued unfaithfulness. God is no longer there. Despite God's absence, the book of Ezekiel ends on a note of tremendous hope, predicting a time of restoration, when "the name of the city from that time on will be: THE LORD IS THERE."

Studying the Name

1. British preacher Charles Spurgeon once said that "whenever it can be said of an assembly, 'The Lord is there,' *unity will be created and fostered.* Show me a church that quarrels, a church that is split up into cliques, a church that is divided with personal ambitions, contrary doctrines, and opposing schemes, and I am sure that the Lord is not there." How have you experienced unity as a mark of God's presence in your church and in your home?
2. What are other marks of God's presence?
3. What is the connection between keeping God's laws and living in his presence?
4. How do you experience God's presence in your life?

Tuesday

PRAYING THE NAME

When you pass through the waters,
I will be with you;
and when you pass through the rivers,
they will not sweep over you.
When you walk through the fire,
you will not be burned;
the flames will not set you ablaze. (Isaiah 43:2)

Reflect On: Isaiah 43:2
Praise God: That he is always with us.
Offer Thanks: For God's presence in the midst of trouble.
Confess: Any tendency to conclude that you are alone in your struggles.
Ask God: To protect you and your loved ones.

Have you ever sat across the table from someone who shouldn't even be walking around on the planet? A year ago I met a woman named Genelle Guzman-McMillan. Her story mesmerized me because she survived troubles the rest of us have only encountered in our nightmares. She is the last survivor of the September 11 attack on the World Trade Center.

Genelle is a soft-spoken woman who remembers what happened in terrifying detail. Employed by the Port Authority of New York, she arrived a little after 8 a.m. on September 11 and rode the elevator to her job on the sixty-fourth floor of the north tower. Thinking it was safe to stay, Genelle didn't attempt to leave the building until after the second plane hit. Racing down fifty-one flights of stairs in high heels, she stopped for a moment on the thirteenth floor. As she bent down to remove her shoes, the north tower collapsed on top of her.

Like millions of others, I watched the horrifying scene via live TV, convinced that no one had survived the collapse of the second tower.

Here's what happened to Genelle when all hell broke loose:

> One hundred ten floors were coming down around us. I knew I was being buried alive. The noise was deafening....
>
> When I woke again I told myself I had to do something. But what could I do? "God, you've got to help me!" I prayed. "You've got to show me a sign, show me a miracle, give me a second chance. Please save my life!" My eyes were so caked with grime that the tears couldn't come, but I felt it in my heart. I was talking to God as though he were right there. I told him I was ready to live my life the right way. "Lord, just give me a second chance, and I promise I will do your will." ...
>
> The next day I heard a beep-beep sound like a truck backing up. I called for help, but there was no response.... Finally someone hollered back: "Hello, is somebody there?" "Yes, help me! My name is Genelle, and I'm on the thirteenth floor," I cried, not realizing how ludicrous the information about my location must have sounded, coming from a pile of rubble....
>
> I could see a bit of daylight coming through a crack, so I stuck my hand through it.... I stretched my hand out as far as I could, and this time someone grabbed it. "Genelle, I've got you! You're going to be all right. My name is Paul. I won't let go of your hand until they get you out."

Genelle had prayed to the God she had ignored for most of her life, and he had been there for her. After twenty-seven hours she was pulled out of the rubble and then spent five weeks in the hospital recuperating. Afterward, she tried locating Paul, the man who had held onto her hand until she was rescued. Later, when she asked about him, her rescuers assured her: "There's no one named Paul on our team . . . nobody was holding your hand when we were removing the rubble."

Genelle had felt completely calm the moment Paul grabbed her hand. She had believed his repeated assurances that help was on the way and that she would be all right. Despite the fact that her story has been told in Jim Cymbala's book *Breakthrough Prayer*, on *Oprah* and *CNN*, and in *Guideposts* and *Time* magazines, no one named Paul has ever stepped forward to take credit for rescuing her. But Genelle knows that Paul was there. He was like an angel of God's presence, assuring her that all would be well.

Hour after hour Genelle had cried out for help. It took more than a day for the rescue crew to locate her but only an instant for God to pinpoint her location. When a psychiatrist, probing for symptoms of posttraumatic stress, interviewed her in the hospital, Genelle told him that God above was her psychiatrist. "After all, God was there when I needed him. He had made sure I was found. He had comforted me and given me a new life." Like few others, Genelle knows the saving power of the One who revealed himself to her as *Yahweh Shammah,* the Lord who is there.

Wednesday

PRAYING THE NAME

In all their distress he too was distressed,
and the angel of his presence saved them.
In his love and mercy he redeemed them;
he lifted them up and carried them
all the days of old. (Isaiah 63:9)

Even the darkness will not be dark to you;
the night will shine like the day,
for darkness is as light to you. (Psalm 139:12)

Reflect On:	Isaiah 63:9 and Psalm 139
Praise God:	For his compassion.
Offer Thanks:	For God's presence in your life.
Confess:	Any tendency to accuse God of abandoning you.
Ask God:	To reveal the ways he has been with you even in times of darkness.

Philip Yancey's book *Where Is God When It Hurts?* is a perennial best-seller, in part because it hits a nerve. Pain and suffering can damage our faith. Throw us headlong into confusion. Convince us we are motherless children left to fend for ourselves. Almost as bad as the thought of God abandoning us is the notion that he is standing by but with a look of disapproval on his face, with an "I told you so" kind of expression, as if to say that we are only getting what we deserve.

The other day a close friend confided that she and her husband were having difficulty. Dan had suffered irreversible brain damage after a motorcycle accident two years earlier. Since then, he'd become irritable and impulsive, hard to get along with. The two had regular shouting matches. They lived in a constant state of tension. Nothing seemed to help. Not the medicine, not the therapy, not the prayers, not all the effort or goodwill in the world. The loving, mature man Jennifer had known for the first ten years of their married life was gone for good. She found it hard to like Dan, let alone to love him.

Jennifer's suffering was compounded by her sense of guilt. She chided herself for reacting so poorly to him. Why couldn't she be more patient, more understanding? The poor man had been in an accident! She could feel God's displeasure. Then she stumbled on Isaiah 63:9.

> *In all their distress he too was distressed,*
> *and the angel of his presence saved them.*
> *In his love and mercy he redeemed them;*
> *he lifted them up and carried them*
> *all the days of old.*

This picture of God took her by surprise, suddenly altering the picture she had formulated in her own mind. Instead of seeing Dan and herself at odds while a disapproving God looked on, she saw the three of them together. All three were weeping. All three were grieving what had happened to Dan and to their marriage. She no longer felt divine disapproval but divine compassion. God was standing beside her, sharing her distress.

By transforming her picture of the spiritual reality, God was beginning to transform her understanding of the possibilities for her marriage. The answers might not be swift. They might not be exactly what she had hoped. But there would be relief because God was there, present in the midst of her suffering. Jennifer remembered the words of her favorite psalm: "For even the darkness will not be dark to you; the night will shine like the day, for darkness is as light to you."

Jennifer's story helped me. I thought about how a single Scripture passage had transformed her sense of how God looked at her. Today, as you face your own set of struggles, join me in reading the words of Isaiah as though God is speaking them directly to you:

In all their distress he too was distressed,
and the angel of his presence saved them.
In his love and mercy he redeemed them;
he lifted them up and carried them
all the days of old.

Thursday

Praying the Name

Then the Lord said to me: "Even if Moses and Samuel were to stand before me, my heart would not go out to this people. Send them away from my presence! Let them go!" (Jeremiah 15:1)

Then he will say to those on his left, "Depart from me, you who are cursed, into the eternal fire prepared for the devil and his angels. For I was hungry and you gave me nothing to eat, I was thirsty and you gave me nothing to drink, I was a stranger and you did not invite me in, I needed clothes and you did not clothe me, I was sick and in prison and you did not look after me." (Matthew 25:41–43)

Reflect On: Jeremiah 15:1 and Matthew 25:31–46
Praise God: For his presence in your life.
Offer Thanks: For the ways God has revealed himself to you.
Confess: Any neglect of the poor and needy.
Ask God: To make you an instrument of his love, revealing his presence through your acts of kindness.

If someone asked you who said the most terrifying words in the Bible, how would you answer? Would you cite one of the prophets? Perhaps Isaiah, Jeremiah, or Ezekiel, who thundered on about fire, famine, conquest, doom, and calamity? Would you go back to the beginning, quoting God himself in Genesis' account of Adam and Eve's expulsion from Paradise?

It might not occur to you that the most terrifying words of all are spoken not in the Hebrew Scriptures but in the New Testament, and they are spoken not by some stern prophet but by Jesus himself: "Depart from me." Three little words that sum up the worst of all fears. Why? Because they describe hell, define damnation. To be cast out of paradise with no hope of return is to be separated from God forever. Abandoning God, we find ourselves abandoned. Instead of *Yahweh Shammah,* we hear "God is *not* there." Instead of *Immanuel* ("God with us"), we hear, "God is *not* with you." When we lose God, we lose hope, love, mercy, faith, kindness, beauty, joy, happiness, comfort, pleasure, strength, wonder, justice, goodness, friendship, peace, protection, understanding, tenderness. You can make up your own list of all the good things that would be subtracted from your life were there no trace of God in it.

But why entertain such thoughts? Because, to paraphrase the words of an old song, we don't know what we've got 'til it's gone. We don't realize the benefits of air, for instance, until we are deprived of it for even a few seconds. If you want to grasp the importance of something, it may help to consider what life would be like without it.

Don't take my word for it. Spend ten minutes today imagining even a day of your life without God in it. Then spend ten minutes calling to mind all the blessings of his presence you regularly take for granted. Remember, too, that God's presence in your life should overflow into the world around you. Do what you can while you can to feed the hungry, welcome strangers, clothe the poor, heal the sick, and care for those in prison. As you do, you will understand more deeply the words spoken by Ezekiel more than five hundred years before the birth of Christ: "And the name of the city from that time on will be: THE LORD IS THERE."

Friday

Promises Associated with God's Name

Immanuel, "God with us"—Jesus is the greatest of all the promises of God. In him God's promise to dwell with his people is fulfilled in a way that is more astonishing than anything we could have imagined. But there is more. We are not only to dwell with God but to be indwelt by him through the power of the Holy Spirit. The book of Revelation envisions a new Jerusalem composed of all the faithful who will forever be united with Christ in the most intimate relationship we can imagine—as bride and bridegroom.

Promises in Scripture

"The virgin will be with child and will give birth to a son, and they will call him Immanuel"—which means, "God with us." (Matthew 1:23)

Consequently, you are no longer foreigners and aliens, but fellow citizens with God's people and members of God's household, built on the foundation of the apostles and prophets, with Christ Jesus himself as the chief cornerstone. In him the whole building is joined together and rises to become a holy temple in the Lord. And in him you too are being built together to become a dwelling in which God lives by his Spirit. (Ephesians 2:19–22)

Then I saw a new heaven and a new earth, for the first heaven and the first earth had passed away, and there was no longer any sea. I saw the Holy City, the new Jerusalem, coming down out of heaven from God, prepared as a bride beautifully dressed for her husband. And I heard a loud voice from the throne saying, "Now the dwelling of God is with men, and he will live with them. They will be his people, and God himself will be with them and be their God. He will wipe every tear from their eyes. There will be no more death or mourning or crying or pain, for the old order of things has passed away." (Revelation 21:1–4)

Continued Prayer and Praise

Remember that God's Presence led his people out of slavery. (Exodus 33:12–17)

Imagine how the glory of the Lord filled the temple. (2 Chronicles 6:41–42; 7:1–3)

Know that God desires to dwell with us. (Psalm 132:13–16)

Be glad, for God will live among us. (Zechariah 2:10–13)

Rejoice because God is pleased to dwell in all fullness in Jesus. (Colossians 1:15)

Remember that the Son is the radiance of God's glory and the exact representation of his being. (Hebrew 1:1–3)

Realize that we are God's temple. (1 Corinthians 3:16)

26

FATHER

אָב αββα πατήρ

AB, ABBA, PATER

The Name

Though the Old Testament provides many rich names and titles for God, the New Testament reveals him most fully. Jesus, in fact, shocked and offended the religious leaders of his day by claiming that he had a Father/Son relationship with the God whose name they feared even to pronounce. Furthermore, by inviting his followers to call God "Father," he made this the primary name by which God is to be known to his followers. That's why we can boldly pray the prayer Jesus taught his disciples, "Our Father who art in heaven. . . ."

Key Scripture

While he was still a long way off, his father saw him and was filled with compassion for him; he ran to his son, threw his arms around him and kissed him. (Luke 15:20)

Monday

GOD REVEALS HIS NAME

Now the tax collectors and "sinners" were all gathering around to hear him. But the Pharisees and the teachers of the law muttered, "This man welcomes sinners and eats with them." . . .

Jesus continued: "There was a man who had two sons. The younger one said to his father, 'Father, give me my share of the estate.' So he divided his property between them.

"Not long after that, the younger son got together all he had, set off for a distant country and there squandered his wealth in wild living. After he had spent everything, there was a severe famine in the whole country, and he began to be in need. So he went and hired himself out to a citizen of that country, who sent him to his fields to feed pigs. He longed to fill his stomach with the pods that the pigs were eating, but no one gave him anything.

"When he came to his senses, he said, 'How many of my father's hired men have food to spare, and here I am starving to death! I will set out and go back to my father and say to him: Father, I have sinned against heaven and against you. I am no longer worthy to be called your son; make me like one of your hired men.' So he got up and went to his father.

"But while he was still a long way off, his father saw him and was filled with compassion for him; he ran to his son, threw his arms around him and kissed him.

"The son said to him, 'Father, I have sinned against heaven and against you. I am no longer worthy to be called your son.'

"But the father said to his servants, 'Quick! Bring the best robe and put it on him. Put a ring on his finger and sandals on his feet. Bring the fattened calf and kill it. Let's have a feast and celebrate. For this son of mine was dead and is alive again; he was lost and is found.' So they began to celebrate.

"Meanwhile, the older son was in the field. When he came near the house, he heard music and dancing. So he called one of the servants and asked him what was going on. 'Your brother has come,' he replied, 'and your father has killed the fattened calf because he has him back safe and sound.'

"The older brother became angry and refused to go in. So his father went out and pleaded with him. But he answered his father, 'Look! All these years I've been slaving for you and never disobeyed your orders. Yet you never gave me even a young goat so I could celebrate with my friends. But when this son of yours who has squandered your property with prostitutes comes home, you kill the fattened calf for him!'

"'My son,' the father said, 'you are always with me, and everything I have is yours. But we had to celebrate and be glad, because this brother of yours was dead and is alive again; he was lost and is found.'" (Luke 15:1–2, 11–32)

Father, thank you for loving me even when I was "still a long way off." You showed your gracious, fatherly love even when I bore little resemblance to you. Strengthen my identity as your child and help me to glorify your name by reflecting your character. Amen.

Understanding the Name

The Hebrew Scriptures normally depict God, not as the Father of individuals but as Father to his people, Israel. Pious Jews, aware of the gap between a holy God and sinful human beings, would never have dared address God as *Ab* (Hebrew) or *Abba,* the Aramaic word for "Daddy," which gradually came to mean "dear father." Jesus shocked many of his contemporaries by referring to God as his Father and by inviting his followers to call God "Father." Rather than depicting God as a typical Middle Eastern patriarch who wielded considerable power within the family, he depicted him primarily as a tender and compassionate father, who extends grace to both the sinner and the self-righteous.

The most frequent term for "father" in the New Testament was the Greek word *pater*. The first recorded words of Jesus, spoken to his earthly parents, are these: "Didn't you know I had to be in my Father's house?" (Luke 2:49). In John's gospel, Jesus calls God his Father 156 times. The expression "*Abba, Pater*" (AB-ba pa-TAIR) is found three times in the New Testament, all in prayer. It is the form Jesus used in his anguished cry in Gethsemane: "*Abba,* Father, everything is possible for you. Take this cup from me. Yet not what I will, but what you will" (Mark 14:36).

Studying the Name

1. Who is Jesus speaking to when he tells the story of the wayward son? What might be a counterpart audience in our world?
2. How have you experienced the kind of grace this father extended to his son?
3. Why do you think the wayward son fails to offer to become one of his father's hired servants, as he had planned? (verses 21–22)
4. How is grace offered to both the law breaker and the law keeper in this story?
5. With whom do you most identify in this story? Why?
6. Jesus does not tell us how the older son responds to his father's explanation. Why do you think the story is left open-ended?
7. What does this parable reveal about our heavenly Father?

Tuesday

Praying the Name

"But while he was still a long way off, his father saw him and was filled with compassion for him; he ran to his son, threw his arms around him and kissed him. . . .

"The older brother became angry and refused to go in. . . .

" 'My son,' the father said, 'you are always with me, and everything I have is yours. But we had to celebrate and be glad, because this brother of yours was dead and is alive again; he was lost and is found.' " (Luke 15:20, 28, 31–32)

Reflect On: Luke 15:1–2, 11–32
Praise God: For his generous, fatherly love.
Offer Thanks: That God is not only our King and Lord but also our Father.
Confess: Any attempts to earn your way into the Father's good graces.
Ask God: To reveal himself as Father.

If you want to perceive who God the Father is, earthly models will fail you. Far better to read the parable Jesus told an audience composed of both sinners and self-righteous religious leaders, two groups that had much in common though they would not have thought so. Jesus offers both a stunning portrait of a father who responds to the appalling behavior of two sons in ways no Middle Eastern patriarch would have.

In Jesus' time the Jewish community had a way of punishing sons who lost the family inheritance, squandering it among Gentiles. Angry villagers would gather together to conduct what was known as a *qetsatsah* ceremony, a ritual that consisted of filling a large pot with burned nuts and burned corn and then breaking it in front of the guilty party. As the earthenware pot shattered, the villagers would shout: "So-and-so is cut off from his people." That would be the cue for the errant son to get out of town for good.

Remarkably, the father in Jesus' story failed to act as his listeners expected. Instead of waiting at home for his profligate son to come crawling back, as any dignified Middle Eastern father would have done, the father in Jesus' story keeps a lookout for him. As soon as he spots him, he runs out and throws his arms around his wayward son, showering him with kisses. By acting quickly and with so much tenderness, the father effectively prevents his neighbors from organizing a *qetsatsah* ceremony to cut off his son. Kenneth Bailey, a theologian who has lived most of his life in the Middle East, explains how astonishing such a sight would have been:

> Traditional Middle Easterners, wearing long robes, do not run in public. They never have. To do so would be deeply humiliating. The father runs knowing that in so doing he will deflect the attention of the community away from his ragged son to himself. People will focus on the extraordinary sight of a distinguished, self-respecting landowner humiliating himself in public by running down the road revealing his legs.

But what of the older son, angered by his father's acceptance of his foolish younger brother? Once again, Jesus depicts the father in a way that would have surprised his listeners. Instead of slapping his son and publicly rebuking him for refusing to attend the celebration, the father humbles himself by leaving the feast in order to reach out to his angry son.

Both sons, one a law breaker and the other a law keeper, had publicly offended their father by their selfish behavior. Both were offered not what they deserved but what they needed—extraordinary grace from the father who loved them.

Ask yourself today whether you are more like the older or the younger of these sons. Then thank God for treating you not as you deserve to be treated but as a child worthy of his faithful, fatherly love.

Wednesday

Praying the Name

My sheep listen to my voice; I know them, and they follow me. I give them eternal life, and they shall never perish . . . no one can snatch them out of my Father's hand. I and the Father are one. (John 10:27–30)

The eternal God is your refuge,
and underneath are the everlasting arms.
(Deuteronomy 33:27)

Reflect On:	John 10:27–30; Deuteronomy 33:27
Praise God:	For his promise to watch over you.
Offer Thanks:	For the gift of eternal life.
Confess:	Any failure to take the risks that faith requires.
Ask God:	For the grace to see yourself as his child.

Not long ago, I took my children to a circus billed as "The Greatest Show on Earth." We loved the pageantry and pomp of this three-ring circus, whose talented performers never failed to entertain. I particularly enjoyed the trapeze artists, especially when they performed with a net stretched out beneath them. Without it I found myself preoccupied by the possibility that even a slight mistake might produce fatal results. The tension I felt made it hard to relax as I watched them flying through the air with the greatest of ease.

Afterward, it occurred to me that those who belong to God have an even better safety net, one that never wears out and that prevents them from making fatal spiritual mistakes. Scripture reminds us of this truth by assuring us that "underneath are the everlasting arms." God is cradling us, keeping us safe for an eternity lived in his presence.

Sigmund Freud once wrote that one of the strongest needs of childhood is the need for a father's protection. Fortunately, even those of us whose earthly fathers failed to provide this sense of security can experience God's faithful fatherly protection.

Knowing that the Father will keep our souls safe means we can put our energy not into building up our sense of self but into building up his kingdom. Secure in his arms, we can learn to take the risks that faith requires. If you have been playing it safe, resisting some new direction in your life that you know to be right, take some time today to meditate on God's faithfulness. Tell him you want his will more than you want your own. Then go ahead and do whatever the Father asks!

Thursday

PRAYING THE NAME

Our Father in heaven,
hallowed be your name,
your kingdom come,
your will be done
on earth as it is in heaven.
Give us today our daily bread. (Matthew 6:9–11)

Reflect On:	Matthew 6:9–13
Praise God:	For his ability to bring good out of evil.
Offer Thanks:	For the way God has already provided for you.
Confess:	Any lack of zeal for God's kingdom.
Ask God:	To make doing his will your first and greatest goal.

In the first two sentences of his now famous prayer, Jesus inextricably linked God the Father to our need for daily bread, for daily provision.

Lalani is a Sri Lankan woman who knows what it means to depend on God to provide for her. In 1986 she married Lionel Jayahsinghe, a former Buddhist monk who had converted to Christianity after reading a tract. Shortly after their marriage the two began a small house church despite the opposition of local monks who went door to door warning people against them. It wasn't long before Lionel started receiving death threats. One Friday in March 1988 Lalani heard a gunshot. Lionel had been shot in the face. Her husband stumbled into their bedroom, followed by an assailant who stabbed him repeatedly. As she turned away to shelter her eleven-month-old son, she heard another gunshot.

After Lionel's death, Lalani became determined to continue the work they had begun in their home, despite threats against her own life. During the years that followed, the church grew despite continued opposition. At one point the roof was burned and later on, in 1999, the church property was bombed. Today, there are 1,200 believers who attend the church that she and her husband founded.

Not long ago, Lalani traveled to another city for a planning meeting with other Christian leaders.

> When asked how things were with her church, she replied, "Wonderful! Praise the Lord!" Later she gave a more detailed report, telling how the local opposition had that week organized a protest march against her church, and then burned the thatch roof.
>
> Stunned by this news, someone in the meeting asked why she said that everything was wonderful. "Obviously," she answered enthusiastically, "since the thatch is gone, God must intend to give us a metal roof!"

What a remarkable statement! Instead of complaining about her hardships, Lalani praised God because she fully expected her heavenly Father to turn these difficulties into a blessing for the church. Today take time to reflect on the faith of this remarkable woman and ask God to increase your own zeal for his kingdom and your faith in his ability to provide for you.

Friday

Promises Associated with God's Name

What a stunning revelation—that God is not only Lord and Master, the Ancient of Days, the Mighty Creator, the Holy One of Israel, but also Abba. And we are his children, not by virtue of our humanity but by adoption into his family. Because of Jesus our Brother, we dare to call God Father, to count on his compassion, to depend on his provision, to lean on his love.

Promises in Scripture

A father to the fatherless, a defender of widows,
is God in his holy dwelling.
God sets the lonely in families,
he leads forth the prisoners with singing. (Psalm 68:5–6)

As a father has compassion on his children,
so the LORD has compassion on those who fear him;
for he knows how we are formed,
he remembers that we are dust. (Psalm 103:13–14)

See how the lilies of the field grow. They do not labor or spin. Yet I tell you that not even Solomon in all his splendor was dressed like one of these. If that is how God clothes the grass of the field which is here today and tomorrow is thrown into the fire, will he not much more clothe you, O you of little faith? So do not worry, saying, "What shall we eat?" or "What shall we drink?" or "What shall we wear?" For the pagans run after all these things, and your heavenly Father knows that you need them. (Matthew 6:28–32)

Do not be afraid, little flock, for your Father has been pleased to give you the kingdom. (Luke 12:32)

I will be a Father to you,
and you will be my sons and daughters,
says the Lord Almighty. (2 Corinthians 6:18)

Continued Prayer and Praise

Remember that God was like a father to Israel. (Hosea 11:2)

Ask God for the grace to reflect his character. (Matthew 5:43–48)

Praise God, who is the Father of compassion and the God of all comfort. (2 Corinthians 1:3)

Thank God for calling you to be his child. (1 John 3:1–2)

Source Notes

Chapter 2. The God Who Sees Me

Page 36. This story is drawn from Wendy Murray Zoba, "The Hidden Slavery," *Christianity Today* (November 2003), 68–74, and Wendy Murray Zoba, "Finding the 'Real God,'" *Christianity Today* (November 2003), 70–71.

Page 36. Zoba, "Finding the 'Real God,'" 71.

Page 36. Ken Kolker and John Agar, "Slain Prostitute Caught in Global Crime Web," *Grand Rapids Press* (January 8, 2004), 1.

Chapter 5. The Lord Will Provide

Page 71. Alexander MacClaren, *Expositions of Holy Scripture*, vol. 1 (Grand Rapids: Baker, 1974), as quoted in Warren W. Wiersbe, *Classic Sermons on the Names of God* (Grand Rapids: Kregel, 1993), 106.

Chapter 8. The Lord Who Heals

Page 102. S. E. Massengill, *A Sketch of Medicine and Pharmacy* (Bristol, Tenn.: Massengill, 1943), 16, as quoted in S. I. McMillen, *None of These Diseases* (Grand Rapids: Revell, 1963), Spire Books ed., 9.

Page 102. P. E. Adolph, "Healing, Health," in *Zondervan Pictorial Encyclopedia of the Bible*, ed. Merrill C. Tenney (Grand Rapids: Zondervan, 1975), 3:56–58.

Chapter 9. The Lord My Banner

Page 118. The patriarchs and heads of churches in Jerusalem, "Easter Message 2002," posted March 28, 2002, *Worldwide Faith News*, www.wfn.org. Accessed June 27, 2003.

Chapter 10. Consuming Fire, Jealous God

Page 122. Edward Mac, "God, Names of," in James Orr, ed., *The International Standard Bible Encyclopedia* (Grand Rapids: Eerdmans, 1939), 2:1267.

Page 125. Taken from the World Watch List, released January 2003 by Open Doors, an international organization founded by Brother Andrew to strengthen the persecuted church throughout the world.

Page 126. See World Watch List at www.opendoors.org.au. Accessed May 24, 2004.

Page 127. Ignatius of Antioch, Eph. 11:1; cf. *Theological Dictionary of the New Testament,* ed. G. Kittel and G. Friedrich, trans. G. W. Bromiley (Grand Rapids: Eerdmans, 1967), 5:446.

Page 130. Joseph Addison, as quoted in *And I Quote,* compiled by Ashton Applewhite, William R. Evans III, and Andrew Frothingham (New York: St. Martin's, 1992), 137.

Chapter 11. Holy One of Israel

Page 138. Addison H. Leitch, "Righteousness," *Zondervan Pictorial Encyclopedia of the Bible,* ed. Merrill C. Tenney (Grand Rapids: Zondervan, 1975), 5:105.

Page 140. C. S. Lewis, *The Magician's Nephew* (New York: HarperCollins, 1955), 125–27 (chs. 9–10).

Chapter 13. The Lord of Hosts

Page 164. German text by Martin Luther, translated into English by Frederick H. Hedge.

Page 165. For the story of Jacob read Genesis 25:19–34; 27–33.

Page 165. George Campbell Morgan, *The Westminster Pulpit,* vol. 9 (London: Pickering and Inglis), as quoted in Warren W. Wiersbe, *Classic Sermons on the Names of God,* compiled by Warren W. Wiersbe (Grand Rapids: Kregel, 1993), 33.

Page 165. Ibid., 34.

Chapter 15. The Lord Is My Shepherd

Page 191. A. B. "Banjo" Paterson, "The Merino Sheep." Posted on website of the University of Queensland Australia: www.uq.edu.au/~mlwham/banjo/three_elephant_power/the_merino_sheep.html. Accessed May 24, 2004.

Chapter 20. Dwelling Place, Refuge, Shield, Fortress, Strong Tower

Page 247. Joedafi, "Liberian Refugee Escapes Death by a Miracle." Posted by SOON Online Magazine at www.soon.org.uk/liberia.htm. Accessed May 24, 2004.

Chapter 21. Judge

Page 262. Eddie's story is told by the Innocence Project, http://www.innocenceproject.org/case/display_profile.php?id+110. Accessed May 24, 2004.

Page 262. See also Psalm 72:1–14; 82:1–8; Jeremiah 22:16; Amos 5:12–15; Micah 3:9–12; Matthew 25:34–45.

Chapter 22. Hope of Israel

Page 277. The study was conducted by Stephen L. Stern, M.D., of the department of psychiatry at the University of Texas Health Science Center at San Antonio and is briefly described in *Aetna InteliHealth* at http://www.intelihealth.com/IH/ihtIH/WSIHW000/333/8014/322301l.html. Accessed February 2004.

Page 277. Felicia in *Finishing Touches,* Act 3.

Chapter 23. The Lord Our Righteousness

Page 282. Addison H. Leitch, "Righteousness," *Zondervan Pictorial Encyclopedia of the Bible*, ed. Merrill C. Tenney (Grand Rapids: Zondervan, 1975), 5:115.

Page XXX. John Henry Newman, *Prayers, Poems, Meditations* (London: SPCK), as quoted in *Magnificat* (December 2003), 201.

Chapter 24. God Most High

Page XXX. Elmer L. Towns, *My Father's Name* (Ventura, Calif.: Regal, 1991), 58.

Chapter 25. The Lord Is There

Page 298. Charles H. Spurgeon, *The Metropolitan Tabernacle Pulpit,* vol. 37, as quoted in *Classic Sermons on the Names of God,* compiled by Warren W. Wiersbe (Grand Rapids: Kregel, 1993), 20.

Page 306. Genelle Guzman-McMillan's story is told in Jim Cymbala, *Breakthrough Prayer* (Grand Rapids: Zondervan, 2003), 67, 69–70.

Page 309. Ibid, 73.

Chapter 26. Father

Page 322. Kenneth E. Bailey, *Jacob and the Prodigal* (Downers Grove, Ill.: InterVarsity Press, 2003), 102.

Page 322. Ibid., 109.

Page 327. Tim Stafford, "The Joy of Suffering in Sri Lanka," christianitytoday.com/ct/2003/010/5.54.html. Accessed May 24, 2004.

Selected Bibliography

Arthur, Kay. *Lord, I Want to Know You.* Colorado Springs: Waterbrook, 1992, 2000.

Barker, Kenneth L., and John Kohlenberger III, eds. *Zondervan NIV Bible Commentary.* 2 vols. Grand Rapids: Zondervan, 1994.

Brown, Colin, ed. *New International Dictionary of New Testament Theology.* 4 vols. Grand Rapids: Zondervan, 1986.

Bruce, F. F., ed. *The International Bible Commentary.* Grand Rapids: Zondervan, 1986.

Douglas, J. D., and Merrill C. Tenney, eds. *The New International Dictionary of the Bible.* Grand Rapids: Zondervan, 1963, 1964, 1967, 1987.

Freedman, David Noel, ed. *The Anchor Bible Dictionary.* 6 vols. New York: Doubleday, 1992.

Hemphill, Ken. *The Names of God.* Nashville: Broadman & Holman, 2001.

Lockyer, Herbert. *All the Divine Names and Titles in the Bible.* Grand Rapids: Zondervan, 1975.

Richards, Larry. *Every Name of God in the Bible.* Nashville: Thomas Nelson, 2001.

Richards, Lawrence O. *New International Encyclopedia of Bible Words.* Grand Rapids: Zondervan, 1999.

Stone, Nathan. *Names of God.* Chicago: Moody Press, 1944.

Tenney, Merrill C., ed. *Zondervan Pictorial Encyclopedia of the Bible.* 5 vols. Grand Rapids: Zondervan, 1975, 1976.

Towns, Elmer L. *My Father's Names.* Ventura, Calif.: Regal, 1991.

VanGemeren, Willem A. *New International Dictionary of Old Testament Theology and Exegesis.* 5 vols. Grand Rapids: Zondervan, 1997.

Wiersbe, Warren W., ed. *Classic Sermons on the Names of God.* Grand Rapids: Kregel, 1993.

ALSO AVAILABLE:

Praying the Names of God Journal

A wonderful companion to the Zondervan trade book, *Praying the Names of God*, by Ann Spangler, the journal will follow the same format as found in the book: a full week of guided journaling space for each of the twenty-six Hebrew names of God. This reflective journal will draw each user into an intimate time of reflection and awe.

Hardcover: 0-310-80846-4